MILITARY FLAGS
OF THE WORLD
in color
1618–1900

MILITARY FLAGS
OF THE WORLD

in color

TERENCE WISE

Illustrated by Guido Rosignoli

ARCO PUBLISHING COMPANY, INC.

NEW YORK

Published 1978 by Arco Publishing Company, Inc.
219 Park Avenue South, New York, N.Y. 10003

Copyright © Blandford Press Ltd 1977

Printed in Great Britain

Library of Congress Cataloging in Publication Data

Wise, Terence.
  Military flags of the world, 1618–1900.

  Includes index.
    1. Standards, Military—History. 2. Flags—History.
I. Rosignoli, Guido, joint author. II. Title.
UC590.W57   355.1′5′0903   77-26286
ISBN 0–668–04472–1
ISBN 0–668–04483–7 pbk.

CONTENTS

THE COLOUR PLATES

The flags are illustrated in chronological order, grouped according to the wars listed below. The numbers are those of the first flag in the group, in both the illustrations and the text.

INTRODUCTION

There are a number of excellent flag books currently available but they deal almost exclusively with national flags, while those specializing in military flags have mostly been out of print for many years, are difficult to obtain and are in the language of the country whose flags they describe. The aim of this book, therefore, is to partly bridge this surprising gap in the study of flags, beginning when the formation known as a regiment came into existence and terminating when military flags were no longer carried into battle as a general rule.

In a book this size, spanning a period of 300 years of history, there is room for only a brief excursion into the subject and for space reasons I have been forced to abandon any hope of listing the official regulations for the military flags of all countries, or even the major countries. I have instead made a selection of flags to be illustrated, the text providing as much information on these flags as space permits.

In my selection of the illustrations I have tried to strike a balance between the more popular flags of the famous regiments of the world and the large number of flags of lesser-known regiments which have either not been illustrated before or have not been available in our time to a wide public. In order to describe the maximum number of flags I have also illustrated as many basic patterns as possible, designs used by all the line cavalry or infantry of a country within a set period of time. This decision was really made for me, as such flags often remained in service for many years, until a new model was introduced – often by a new monarch, and because the colour variations within the basic pattern can be easily listed in a small space. Therefore, although 392 flags are illustrated in the colour plates, and a further fifteen by line drawings, in fact information on just over 900 flags is to be found in this book.

It should also be noted that the dates of many of the wars overlap, while the design of the flags did not necessarily change for each war. This has enabled a wider range of flags for the various arms and nationalities to be illustrated for any given period than would at first appear possible from the number of illustrations within each heading, and readers are advised to look forwards and backwards in both illustrations and text for additional information on any single period. It is hoped the index will help with this.

9

SOURCES

BOOKS

Barraclough, E. M. C. *Flags of the World*. 1971

Blake, M. *American Civil War Cavalry*. 1973
    American Civil War Infantry. 1970

Blount, T. *The Art of Making Devises*. 1650

Brückner, A. and B. *Schweizer Fahnenbuch*. 1942

Bullock, H. *Indian Cavalry Standards*. 1930
    Indian Infantry Colours. 1930

Catalogue of Foreign Colours, Standards and Guidons, Kungl. Armémuseum, Stockholm

Chariol, Bouillé du. *Les Drapeaux Françaises de 507 à 1872*. 1st ed. 1872, 2nd ed. 1875

Chelminski, J. V. and Malibran, A. M. *L'Armée du duché de Varsovie*. 1913

Cox, M. W. *Romantic Flags of Texas*. 1936

Curson, H. H. *Colours and Honours in South Africa*. 1948

Edwards, T. J. *Standards, Guidons and Colours of the Commonwealth Forces*. 1953

Ford, J. *War Flags etc. at Chelsea Hospital*. 1861

Fraser, E. *War Drama of the Eagles*. 1912

Gayre, G. R. *Heraldic Standards*. 1959

German Army. *Die Uniformen und Fahnen der deutschen Armee*. 189(?)

Grouvel, Vicomte. *Les Corps de Troupe L'Émigration Française*. 1957–64

Historische Fahnen. *Die Welt in Bildern Album 8*. 1919(?)

Hollander, O. *Les Drapeaux des Régiments d'Infanterie Française*. 1933

Hulme, F. E. *Flags of the World*. 1908

Kaindl, F. *Von den Gemalten zu den Gewebten Feldzeichen*. 1969

Katcher, P. *Armies of the American Wars, 1753–1815*. 1975

Lemonofides, D. *British Infantry Colours*. 1971
    British Cavalry Standards. 1971

Lerondeau, J. *Au drapeau*. 1953

Lovell, W. *Enseignes of the Regiments in the rebellious Citty of London*. 1643

Maury, A. *Les Emblèmes et les drapeaux de la France*. 1904

Milne, S. M. *Standards and Colours of the Army, 1661–1881*. 1893

Niox, G. L. *Drapeaux et Trophées*. 1910

Pengel, R. and Hurt, G. R. *Flags of the French Infantry during the Seven Years War, Part 1.* 1975
    Prussian and Austro-Hungarian Flags of the Seven Years War. 1976
Rawkins, W. J. *Kingdom of Saxony Infantry Standards, 1810–13.* 1976
Quaife, M. M. *Flags of the United States.* 1942
    History of the United States Flag. 1961
Sales, P. de *Bandeiras e Estandartes.* 1930
Schermerhorn, F. E. *American and French Flags of the Revolution, 1775–1783,* 1948
Smith, Whitney. *Flag Book of the United States.* 1970
    Flags of the American Revolution. 1975
    Flags through the ages and across the world. 1975
Standards taken in the Civil Wars. 1643
Symonds, R. *Diary of the Marches of the Royal Army during the Great Civil War. (1644–5).* 1859
Venn, T. *Military Observations or Tacticks . . .* 1672
Viskovatov, A. V. *Istoricheskoe opisanie odezhdui i vooruzheniya rossiiskikh voisk.* 1899–1902
Zvegintsov, V. V. *Znamena i shtandartui russkoi armii XV–1914.* 1964

JOURNALS AND PERIODICALS

It is not possible to list full details of all the articles read and collected over the years, but various issues of the journals etc. listed below have been consulted and I would like to pay particular acknowledgement to the work done by Commander R. O. Morris R.N., W. Y. Carmen, Piero Crociani and Dino Lemonofides.

Alti Congresso 1st Internazionale, Amatori di Armi; Army Historical Research journal; Army Quarterly; Deutsches Soldatenjahrbuch; Flag Research Center bulletin; King's Royal Rifle Corps Chronicle for 1923; Military Collector and Historian; Military Historical Society journal; Miniature Warfare; Modelworld; National Geographical Magazine, 1934 and 1949; Society Napoleonic journal; Tradition.

MUSEUMS

My sincere thanks to the staffs of the British Library, Victoria and Albert Museum Library, National Army Museum Library and Luzo-Brazilian Council's Library in London, and to the following European institutions: Arquivo Histórico Militar, Lisbon; Musée de l'Armée, Paris; Kungl. Armémuseum, Stockholm; Heeresgeschichtliches Museum, Vienna; Estado-Maior do Exército, Lisbon; Servicio Historico Militar, Madrid.

PERSONAL ACKNOWLEDGEMENTS

I would also like to take this opportunity to record my debt to the following people, who have kindly assisted me in my researches by advice or material from their files: Ignacio de Ribot y de Balle, Mike Blake, Tony Burgess, Fred Feather, Alan Hansford Waters, Furio Lorenzetti, the late Louis Loynes, Louis Muhlemann, Otto von Pivka, W. P. Sellick, Major Peter Walton and Brigadier Peter Young.

Finally I should also like to express my thanks to Barry Gregory of Blandford Press for editing the script and for his diligence in eliminating a number of inconsistencies.

GLOSSARY

charge	the devices placed upon a shield.
chief	the top third of a shield.
cross crosslet	small transverse pieces placed across each arm of a cross to form four small crosses springing from the centre.
dexter	the left side when facing a coat of arms.
escarbuncle	a charge based on the iron strengthening bands radiating from the centre of a shield.
escutcheon	a shield or coat of arms.
fimbriate	a charge given a narrow border of a different hue.
fitchée	generally applied to crosses when their lower arm comes to a point.
fusil	as a lozenge but longer and narrower.
gorged	an animal wearing a collar is said to be gorged.
guardant	looking towards the spectator.
impaled	two coats of arms conjoined vertically are impaled.
in bend	charges following the line taken by the charge known as a bend.
in pale	charges following the line taken by the charge known as a pale.

lozenge	a diamond-shaped charge.
lozengy	a number of lozenges formed by vertical and diagonal lines, as in the Bavarian arms.
overall	a charge borne over another and obscuring part of it, or covering the entire field.
passant	passing or walking.
pile wavy	a wedge-shaped charge known as a pile but with wavy edges.
proper	charges appearing in their natural colour or colours.
quartering	a shield divided into four equal parts by a cross is said to be quartered. The dexter chief is number 1, sinister chief 2, dexter base 3, sinister base 4.
raguly	ragged, as the trunk of a tree with the branches lopped off.
rampant	an animal erect with three paws off the ground and head looking to the dexter.
roundels	small round charges.
saltire	two diagonal bands crossing to form a charge (a St Andrew's cross).
seeded	when the seed of a flower is of a different colour from the petal it is known as seeded.
semée	when a field is strewn with small charges.
sinister	the right side when facing a coat of arms.
statant	an animal standing still with all its legs on the ground.
sun in its splendour	when a sun bears a human face and is surrounded by rays.

tinctures   heraldic term for the various hues employed: Argent = silver or white; Azure = blue; Gules = red; Or = gold or yellow; Sable = black; Vert = green.

Readers wishing to pursue the subject of heraldry further are recommended to start with a handy reference such as the *Observer Book of Heraldry*, published by Warne.

HISTORICAL BACKGROUND

The Evolution of Flags

It is not known when or where the first 'flags' were flown, but they have been carried into battle by almost every known culture of the world since history has been recorded: 'banners' are mentioned extensively in the Old Testament and it is known that streamers were attached to the carved wooden standards of the Egyptians some 3000 years before Christ. Even at this early date the emblems carried into battle followed definite patterns, suggesting they had evolved well before this date. However, these earliest of battle symbols placed the emphasis on a staff with a static object at its top – they were standards not flags: the Egyptian streamers were mere appendages, and it is not known what form the Biblical 'banners' took.

One of the earliest references to a flag, as opposed to a standard, occurs in Chinese records in 1122 B.C., and the first actual record of a flag (for cavalry) is found in the Chinese *Book of War*, written *circa* 500 B.C. The earliest surviving illustration of a flag, again Chinese, is on a tomb and dates from the Han Dynasty (200 B.C. to A.D. 200). These were all true flags in that they were of cloth, probably silk, and were large in size. 'Standards' are recorded in Phoenicia in the fifth century B.C. and it is extremely interesting to learn that the Greeks were using signal flags in naval battles in the same era. All these early references imply that flags, as distinct from standards, developed in the East some 3000 years ago, and that by the fifth century B.C. they had spread to the Mediterranean, with some form of recognized system for their design and use.

From the Mediterranean the use of flags spread northwards to the Roman republic, where the vexillum was adopted for cavalry units. However, the Romans retained the standard for their legions and as a result the development of flags did not make much progress in Europe at this date. The vexillum, suspended from a horizontal cross bar, remained the only true flag in the western world until the ninth century and it was in China, and from there through the Middle East, that the flag developed its intrinsic value as *the* symbol of authority and power, secured laterally to a stave to enable it to flow in the breeze, attracting attention by both its colours and motion.

The Islamic countries of the Middle East had been using standards for many centuries, but it is known that by at least the seventh century A.D. they were also using flags. The Islamic invasion of Spain in the eighth century therefore introduced the laterally attached flag (on lances) to the West, to be copied by the Spaniards and Portuguese.

The first flag in North West Europe to fly from a vertical stave appears about A.D. 878 – the famous raven flag of the Vikings. It is possible that Vikings fighting for the Byzantine emperors took the idea of such flags back to Scandinavia with them. From the Bayeux Tapestry, made between 1070 and 1080, we know for certain that by that date such flags were firmly established in the West, possibly spreading north and east from the Iberian peninsula and south and west from Scandinavia. By the time of the Crusades the use of military flags flying from vertical staves for both infantry and cavalry was universal.

At first there appears to have been little, if any, control over flag types and their use in the West, and a profusion of flags came into being, on lances, castles, ships and for cities; every noble had his own flag, and every knight under him had his large pennon. However, by *circa* 1160 heraldry had evolved and altered the entire nature of flags in the West, not only establishing rules but also to a large extent the designs.

The prime aim of heraldry was to produce simple, instantly recognizable designs, and the types of flags instituted promoted this aim. 'Flag' is a generic term, and in medieval heraldry covered seven main classes:

1. *Pennoncelle* or *Pencel:* the personal flag of a knight, carried on his lance.
2. *Pennon:* the personal flag of a knight bachelor, i.e. an officer responsible for several small formations of men.
3. *Banner:* the personal flag of sovereigns, princes, dukes, earls and barons.
   These first three forms all bore the owner's coat of arms.
4. *Gonfannon:* the Roman vexillum, and rarely used. Often carried by Churchmen or those taking up arms on behalf of the Church.
5. *Streamer:* flown from the masts of ships.
6. *Standard:* a flag used to mark a body of infantry within an army.
7. *Guidon:* a smaller form of standard, carried by the cavalry.

Both the standard and guidon bore the commander's badge or badges, and sometimes his motto or slogan. The badge was worn by the men on their tunics and their commander's standard was therefore instantly identifiable to them, whereas the lord's banner bore his coat of arms, which might not be familiar to all the men under his command.

In the late fifteenth and early sixteenth centuries the art of heraldry began to be debased by over-complex insignia, partly caused by a need to complicate coats of arms because more people were now bearing them, partly the desire to display those arms artistically rather than simply now that their purely functional role had declined. (Shields were no longer carried in battle and individuals and formations were now recognized by their flags.) In the same period there also emerged wars fought between sides divided by religion or ideological differences, and their causes introduced into flag design a great deal of new, non-heraldic symbolism, especially the propaganda type of slogan. These factors brought about the complex, highly artistic, but functionally inferior, military flags typical of the later Renaissance period.

By the late sixteenth century even the shape of flags began to be affected and the heraldic rules ignored. 'Banners' were now carried by infantry as well as cavalry, and for the infantry the banners grew to a far larger size than could ever have been borne by the medieval knight; while some 'standards' became rectangular in shape, losing their long, tapering fly. The large, swallow-tailed pennon became the most common form of cavalry flag in Western Europe during this century, and when dragoons were introduced in the latter part of that century they used a diminished form of this pennon.

Further change was brought about by the growth of standing armies. By the early sixteenth century Continental armies were beginning to abandon their medieval organization; wherein small bodies of men served under a captain, loosely grouped into larger units for battle but retaining divided loyalties and individual flags; and adopted more permanent grouping, such as the Spanish *tercios* and various legions. At this time the term 'regiment' meant little more than a force gathered for a specific task, but during the latter part of the century and early seventeenth century such regiments became permanent and the term came to mean formations of Foot and Horse divided into a regular number of companies and troops, each of which was composed of a definite number of men.

At first the institution of standing armies made little change to the flags carried in battle. The feudal bodies of men raised in particular areas were replaced by bodies of regulars recruited from any part of the kingdom and the commander no longer exercised authority by accident of birth or a knighthood, but as a direct commission from the Crown;

but a colonel ordered to raise a regiment by the king was usually a noble and raised his regiment from his estates, or had some companies raised by his captains from their estates; and therefore the feudal system continued under a different name. This was particularly the case in the cavalry. Mounted troops in the first half of the seventeenth century were still the preserve of the wealthy, and their flags were often rich and complex, bearing among their ornaments the colonel's or captain's badges. For the same reasons infantry flags continued to have a medieval or Renaissance appearance, with each company within a regiment bearing its individual flag.

Gradually the flags began to take on a regimental appearance, just as in the same period – the first half of the seventeenth century – the regiments began to adopt uniform clothing. Each infantry company or cavalry troop had its own flag, but now many began to be in the colour of the men's coats, the various companies and troops distinguished only by heraldic symbols. In some cases the flags of a regiment adopted a basic colour even before the men's coats were of a uniform colour, and such cases occur as late as the 1640s. At the same time several countries adopted a national symbol on their military flags; for example, the white cross of France and the red cross of St George of England, both dating back to the Crusades. Thus at a glance the flag revealed country, regiment and company.

From these humble beginnings the emblem of a nation on its military flags gradually developed, through the struggles for independence and civil wars of the second half of the seventeenth century, until in the revolutionary wars of the late eighteenth and early nineteenth centuries the military flag frequently evolved into the national flag now borne proudly by every country of the world.

The first step towards true regimentation and standardization of military flags as we know them today was probably the division of infantry regiments into three wings – two of musketeers, one of pikemen – early in the seventeenth century. No precise date is known, and probably what followed was a gradual process throughout the century, but as a result of the division of a regiment into three wings, the company flags were eventually abolished and each of the three wings displayed a distinctive flag so that it might act separately from yet remain identifiable as part of the regiment. It is doubtful if any order or regulation was ever issued to this effect.

The next major change was brought about by the introduction of the bayonet at the end of the seventeenth century, thus cancelling the need for pikemen. In the first decades of the eighteenth century, therefore, a regiment was no longer divided into three wings and did not require three flags, and as a general rule the third flag was laid aside. (Examples exist of regiments keeping a third flag until the mid-eighteenth century, but these are exceptions rather than the rule.)

About the same date most European countries began to institute official rules and regulations concerning military flags, although even then there was no great degree of control over the actual colours and standards carried, as each colonel was responsible for the manufacture of his regiment's flags. This situation was not remedied until later in the century when official patterns were drawn up and all flags had to conform to them. Even so variation persisted as late as the early nineteenth century in the interpretation of the patterns until a system for inspecting the flags was instituted.

The first of the two flags of a regiment was now generally known as the Royal, or King's, or Sovereign's colour, and stood for the regiment's allegiance and service to the monarch and nation: to the nation alone in republics. This premier flag was often based on the monarch's arms or the nation's national flag, if it had one at this date. Because the flag was borne by the first company originally, the colonel's company, it is also often referred to as the colonel's colour.

The second flag of a regiment was known as the regimental colour in Britain and North America, as a battalion colour in countries where regiments had more than one battalion. It stood for the soldier's duty to the regiment, and the honour and traditions of the regiment itself.

Flag Terminology

Until now I have tried to avoid referring to military flags of the sixteenth and seventeenth centuries as anything but flags because of the confusion of terms at this period, when the new flag types were evolving. Modern terms for army flags are now generally restricted to:

1. *Standard*, a cavalry flag.
2. *Guidon*, a dragoon or mounted infantry flag.
3. *Colour*, an infantry flag.

These are the terms and their meanings employed throughout this book but it may help to describe briefly the origins of these names, and earlier names no longer in general use but which occur from time to time in older works.

Gayre states in *Heraldic Standards* that in the seventeenth century the long, slender, swallow-tailed standard of medieval times developed a rectangular form, and that this probably led to the development of the square 'banner' which ultimately became the cavalry standard. He goes on to say that rectangular military colours as we know them are also derived from the medieval standard, and that the badges and battle honours borne on them are 'in direct line of descent from the much finer standards of medieval times'.

It will be remembered that the medieval standard was used to identify a large body of infantry on the battlefield and bore the badges of the commander, not his arms. Many standards also bore the nation's symbol in the hoist, for example the cross of St George for England, or the arms of Castile and Leon for Spain. The standard was too large to be borne by a man and was usually carried on a wagon or erected in a suitable spot: a flag made to stand, hence standard. During the Renaissance infantry are portrayed carrying extremely large, square 'banners' on short staves, and the suggestion is therefore that these were derived from the standard. If so, then the smaller, rectangular infantry colours and cavalry standards of the seventeenth century (and many of the former bore national emblems in the canton next to the stave) are certainly direct descendants of the medieval standard, and even today it may be noted that military colours and standards usually bear badges and mottoes, not coats of arms.

It seems logical that standards used to identify large bodies of infantry in medieval times should continue to do so in subsequent centuries, although cut down in length to manageable proportions, i.e. losing the greater part of the fly to become a rectangle or square. It also seems logical to me, though there is no evidence to support the theory, that the medieval square banner, the flag of the noble, would have been used as the flag of a troop of cavalry, raised by that noble, and bear his badge. (Badge-banners did come into use in the fifteenth century, though they were not common, and sometimes banners also had the fringes normally associated with cavalry standards.)

Guidons have always been associated with mounted men, being a smaller form of standard, and carried by the leader of Horse. They were always of the distinctive swallow-tailed shape.

In the fifteenth century pennon-shaped cavalry flags were referred to as cornets (French *cornette*), a term also applied to the flag bearer. Similarly infantry colours were often referred to as ensigns (from insignia or ensignes, the term for armorial bearings on the flags), and a term also applied to the flag bearer. The ranks of ensign and cornet persisted in the British Army until 1871 and 1872 respectively.

The origin of the terms colour and colours is also simple; from the many colours of the early flags; but their coining provides some interesting information on when regimental flags first began to be recognizable as such. The following extracts also show the first formal attempts at rules and regulations for military flags.

From *Certain Discourses* written by Sir John Smythe in 1585: 'Their Ensigns also they will not call by that name but by the name of Colours, which terme is by them so fondly and ignorantly given.'

From the play *Battle of Alcazar* by Peele, performed in 1591:

> 'And now, behold, how Abdelmetic comes,
> Uncle to this unhappy traitor King.
> Arm'd with great aid that Amarath had sent,
> Great Amarath, Emperor of the East,
> For service done to Sultan Soliman,
> Under whose Colours he had served in the field.'

From Barrett's *Theorike and Practike of Modern Warres* published in 1598: 'We Englishmen do call them of late Colours, by reason of the variety of colours they be made of, whereby they be better noted and known.'

By the early seventeenth century the term colours was firmly established and in 1622 Markham attempted to lay down rules in his 'Five Decades of Epistles of Warre':

'Colours ought to be mixed equally of two colours, that is to say, according to the laws of heraldry, of colour and metal.
Captain's Colour: Should consist of the two principal colours in his coat of arms, with a small red cross of St George in the dexter chief canton [i.e. next to the stave head] not larger than one sixth of the entire Colour.
Colonel's Colour: To be the same as the Captain's, but of only one colour throughout.
Colonel-General's and Lord Marshal's Colour: To be the same as the Colonel's but with a smaller St George's cross, only one eighth of the whole Colour.
General's Colour: Of one colour throughout and without any St George's cross.'

Ward's rules (*Animadversions of Warre*, published 1639) are more specific: [office and duty of a Colonel] 'He ought to have all the

Colours of his regiment to be alike both in colour and in fashion to avoid confusion so that soldiers may discern their own Regiment from the other troops; likewise, every particular Captain of his Regiment may have some small distinctions in their Colours; as their Armes, or some Emblem, or the like, so that one company may be discerned from the other.'

In about 1652 Captain Thomas Venn wrote: 'As far as the dignity of an ensign in England (not meddling with the Standard Royal) to a regimental dignity; the colonel's colour, in the first place, is of a pure clean colour, without any mixture. The lieutenant colonel's only with St George's Armes in the upper corner next the staff; the major's the same, but with a little stream blazant [a pile wavy], and every captain with St George's Armes alone, but with so many spots or several devices as pertain to the dignity of their several places.' These words, undoubtedly based on the regimented flags borne in the English Civil Wars, form the first known authority for English colours and, although they were not official regulations as far as we know, they were certainly used as guidelines and were followed closely until the introduction of the first official rules and regulations in the British Army in 1743.

The Design of Flags
As we have seen earlier, military flags really became a branch of heraldry in the medieval period, and should therefore be designed in accordance with the laws of heraldry. For the most part this is the case, but military flags required special features – principally easy identification at a distance – because they were used in battle, and therefore the first consideration should always have been simple designs to enable instant recognition. For example, the heraldic rule of tincture (that no two metals or colours should be placed alongside each other) need not be insisted upon, as this often creates a need for fimbriating (the superimposing of one colour upon another, the bottom colour forming an edging to the upper one) as in the British Union Flag. Similarly, the heraldic terms of dexter and sinister for right and left are not really applicable, and flags have their own terminology.

When describing the various parts of a flag it should be assumed the flag is being held by its stave in the right hand of the flag bearer, who faces the observer with the flag flying over the bearer's head. In this situation the side facing the observer is the obverse, the other or rear side is the reverse: other parts are named on the accompanying illustration. The most honourable part of a flag is next to the stave, in

23

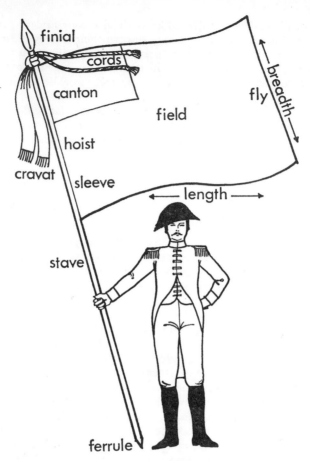

FIG. 1 PARTS OF A FLAG

particular the upper part or canton. Thus the nation's arms or national symbol is often portrayed in this canton.

Flags should ideally be made from pieces of material stitched together, or embroidered on a piece of cloth: they should not be painted as painted flags do not have a very long life. It is noticeable that cavalry standards, which usually saw less active service than infantry colours, were more frequently painted. A flag should also, where possible, be of one thickness of material, so that it remains light and flies well, enabling it to be seen properly. Where the observe and reverse are different then two thicknesses of cloth are obviously necessary. Again, it is more often the cavalry standards, sometimes richly embroidered and fringed, which fall into this category and as a result do not fly well of their own accord. However, because cavalry standards are quite small, a wave of the stave is usually sufficient to display such flags, the weight of the standard actually helping to spread it out in the air.

The Meaning and Value of Flags

The earliest flags and standards were almost always of a religious nature, either sacred symbols to be worshipped, or an emblem which indicated or promoted communication with the gods, and the authority of a flag or standard was initially derived from the power of these religious connexions. The early flags of the French were the oriflamme of St Denis and the blue mantle of St Martin; the Russians bore the symbols of St Andrew and St George; and for centuries the English carried into battle not only the dragon standard of their ancestors but the banners of the Holy Trinity, St George and St Edward the Confessor. Often these banners were carried in the field by monks or ecclesiastics to help inspire confidence in the troops, who were thus led to believe the saints would intervene on their behalf in the coming struggle: Joan of Arc claimed her standard was worth a hundred lances. Today rich banners and gonfannons still play an active part in the ceremonies of some religions (and the 'mystic' societies and trades unions) and through most of modern history the military flags of France and Britain continued to bear the Christian symbol of the cross, a symbol these countries adopted at the time of the Crusades.

The religious flags were often purely pictorial in character, bearing actual representations of the Virgin Mary, Christ, various saints and so forth. These figures were replaced on fighting flags during the medieval period by the symbolism of heraldry, but the Renaissance saw a rebirth of religious symbols on military flags and this type of military flag was especially prevalent during the early part of the Thirty Years War. Thus at the start of our period 'religious' flags were still in common use, and were not fully supplanted until once again heraldic emblems were adopted for regimental flags in the mid-seventeenth century.

From earliest times flags and standards were given religious recognition by some form of consecration and on the Continent in the fourteenth century some simple consecration service appears to have been performed when a new flag was presented. German mercenaries in the late medieval and early Renaissance period took a holy oath to defend their company colour to the death, and some form of consecration ceremony also existed in England by the end of the sixteenth century. Similarly, but from a much later date, there was eventually a 'laying up' service, at which old colours and standards were again blessed by the Church, often followed by preservation in the regiment's local church or a cathedral.

From this it can be seen that flags and standards have always had at least a semi-sacred character, and consequently have always been treated with reverence. But the symbolism of a military flag goes deeper than religion: it is the symbol of the regiment's duty to sovereign and country, of the men's duty to the regiment, and it is this symbolism that men acknowledge when they salute a military flag. It is perhaps not insignificant that at this stage in history, when western people are again beginning to be aware of values other than the purely materialistic, there should be the first signs of an awakening of interest in military flags, whose value is entirely spiritual.

Initially military flags had two simple purposes: to distinguish the forces of the two sides, and to mark in battle the position of the commanders and thus provide rallying points in confused fighting. In an age when men did not wear uniform – and at the start of our period regiments were still distinguished only by sashes or various sprigs of greenery in their hats – flags filled these vital roles and through this came to represent among the confusion of battle the one certain thing to which a soldier could always turn. Sir Charles Napier phrases this best: 'Great is the value of the standard; it is the telegraph in the centre of battle, to speak of changes of the day to the wings. Its importance has therefore been immense in all ages, amongst all nations and in all kinds of wars. "Defend the Colours!" "Form upon the Colours!" is the first cry and first thought of a soldier when any mischance of battle has produced disorder: then do cries, shouts, firing, blows and all combat thicken round the standard; it contains the symbol of the honour of the band, and the brave press round its banner.'

Through the years this fighting round the flag gave it its deeper meaning, its real purpose, for apart from representing authority and unity of purpose, the flags of regiments came to embody the memory of the men who had gone before, the war history and traditions of the regiment, around which the men were loyal unto death, honouring the fallen and protecting the honour of their regiment with their last breath. To allow such a flag to be captured was to dishonour the regiment and all the men who had gone before.

In the nineteenth century it became customary to include the names of battles on the flags, honours granted to regiments for heroism in battle, and such honours were often the only permanent, physical memorial to men who died by their thousands for king, country and regiment. And so a regiment's flag became a symbol, intrinsically valueless, extrinsically priceless, an object through which new men acknowledged their loyalty to those who had given their lives in the past, a living symbol of the spirit and honour of the regiment.

1. Bavaria: von Tilly's Dragoons

2. Friedland-Mecklenburg:
Wallenstein's Life Regt

3. Archduke Leopold's guidon

4. Hessian cavalry standard

5. Saxony: Starschadel Infantry Regt

6. Brunswick cavalry standard

PLATE 1

7. Bavaria:
von Tilly's Infantry Regt

8. Bavarian dragoon guidon

9. Bavarian cavalry standard

10. Elector of Bavaria's standard

11. Spanish cavalry standard

12. Spanish infantry colour

PLATE 2

13. Sweden: Robert Monroe's
Infantry Regt

14. Sweden: Sovereign's colour,
Johan Banér's Life Regt

15. Sweden: cavalry cornet,
Johan Banér's Life Regt

16. Sweden: Johan Forbes' Regt

17. Danish cavalry standard

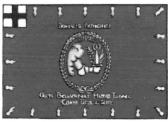

18. Denmark: Frederick III's
Infantry Regt

19. Saxon cavalry standard

20. Saxony:
Franz Albrecht's Regt

PLATE 3

21. Régt de Picardie

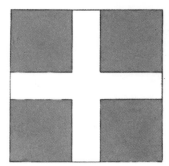

22. Régt de Navarre

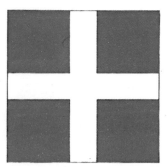

23. Régt de Champagne

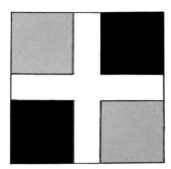

24. Régt d'Auvergne

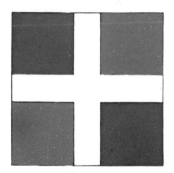

25. Régt de la Marine

26. Les Gardes Écossaises

PLATE 4

27. Polish cavalry guidon

28. King of Poland's
Household troops

29. Polish cavalry standard

30. Cavalry guidon of Tartars
in Polish service

31. Sweden: von Liebenstein's German Regt

32. Sweden: Magnus de la Gardie's
Life Regt

PLATE 5

33. Sweden: Life Regt
of Carl Gustaf

34. Sweden: H.M. Carl XI's
German Guard

36. Russia: Czar's standard

35. Russia: Czar Alexis
Michailovitch's Regt

37. Russia: 12th Regt
Streltzi of Moscow

38. Russia: banner
of the 1645-76 era

PLATE 6

39. Colonel Leveson's
Regt of Horse

40. Lord Hopton's Troop of Guard

41. King's Life Guards

42. Colonel Gerard's
Regt of Foot

43. Colonel Bagott's
Regt of Foot

44. Colonel Taylor's
Regt of Foot

PLATE 7

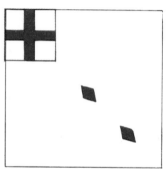

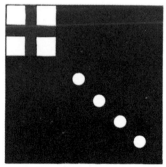

45. Colonel's colour,
Tower Hamlets Regt

46. Major's colour, Orange Regt

47. 1st Captain's colour,
White Regt

48. 2nd Captain's colour,
Green Regt

49. 3rd Captain's colour,
Blue Regt

50. 4th Captain's colour,
Yellow Regt.

PLATE 8

51. Robert, Earl of Essex

52. Essex's Bodyguard

53. Colonel Lambert of Yorkshire

54. 3rd Regt of Dragoons

55. Sir William Sanders
of Buckinghamshire

56. Captain West of Cambridge

PLATE 9

57. Swedish cavalry standard

58. Swedish dragoon guidon

59. Poland: John Casimir's standard

60. Polish cavalry pennon

61. Russian banner
of 1645-76 era

62. Denmark:
Jörgen Rosenkrantz's Regt

PLATE 10

63. France: Régt du Roi

64. France: Régt de Carignan

65. Britain: King's Troop,
Horse Guards

66. Britain: Queen's Troop,
Horse Guards

67. Swedish dragoon guidon

68. Sweden: Viborg Cavalry Regt

PLATE 11

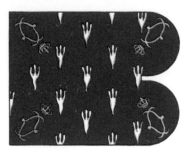

69. France:
Colonel-General of Dragoons

70. France: Dragons d'Orléans

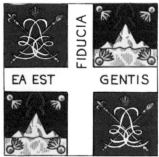

71. France:
Cent-Suisses de la Garde

72. France:
Régt de la Couronne

73. French or Bavarian
infantry colour

74. Britain: King's Own
Royal Regt of Dragoons

PLATE 12

75. Sweden: H.M. German Guard

76. Sweden: August of Saxe-Halle's Infantry Regt

77. King of Denmark's Bodyguard

78. Strasbourg mounted burgher company

79. Brandenburg: Duke Ernst Bogislav Croy's Cavalry Regt

80. Brandenburg: Simon van Bolsey's Marines

PLATE 13

81. H.M. Life Guards

82. Våstmanland company
of the Life Regt

83. Colonel's colour,
H.M. German Life Regt

84. Company colour,
H.M. German Life Regt

85. Västgöta Cavalry Regt

86. Nårke-Värmlands Infantry Regt

PLATE 14

87. Régt de Bourgogne

88. Régt de Bretagne

89. Les Gardes Suisses

90. Colonel Roth's Irish Regt

91. Colonel Bulkeley's Irish Regt

92. Colonel Fitzjames' Irish Regt

PLATE 15

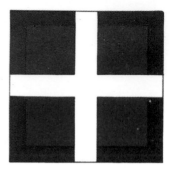

93. France: Régt de Poitou

94. France: Régt de Chartres

95. Holland: Gustaf Mauritz
Lewenhaupt's Regt

96. Holland: infantry colour

97. Savoy: Marine Regt

98. Holy Roman Empire:
infantry colour

PLATE 16

99. Coldstream Regt of Foot Guards

100. 1st Regt of Foot Guards

101. Scots Guards

102. Queen's Troop, Horse Guards

103. Royal Regt of Horse

104. Earl of Shrewsbury's Regt of Horse

PLATE 17

105. Russia: Boris Sheremechev's
Cavalry Regt

106. Russia: Alexis Obuchov's
Infantry Regt

107. Russia: Colonel's colour;
Preobrajenski Life Guards

108. Russia: company colour,
Preobrajenski Life Guards

109. Saxon dragoon guidon

110. Swedish artillery standard

PLATE 18

111. 12th Regt of Foot

112. 1st Royal Regt of Foot

113. Princess Ann of Denmark's Regt

114. 10th Regt of Foot

115. 3rd Regt of Foot

116. Royal Regt of Dragoons

PLATE 19

117. Régt d'Artillerie

118. Régt du Roi

119. Dragons de la Reine

120. Régt de Carmen

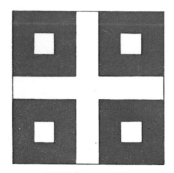

121. Régt de Laffey

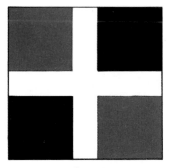

122. Régt de Tiange

PLATE 20

123. Spain: Royal colour
for infantry regts

124. Spain:
Waterford (Irish) Regt

125. Bavarian infantry colour

126. Bavarian cavalry standard

127. Würzburg cavalry standard

128 Prussian infantry colour

PLATE 21

129. Russia: infantry
and dragoon pattern

130. Russia: cuirassier pattern

131. France: Cuirassiers du Roi

132. Austrian hussar standard

133. Saxon cavalry standard

134. Spanish cavalry standard

PLATE 22

135. Spain: Regto de Badajoz

136. Spain: Regto de Melilla

137. Spain: Regto de Valencia

138. France: Hussards de Chamborant

139. France: Gardes Françaises

140. Lübeck Burgerwehr

PLATE 23

141. Prussia: 4th Dragoon Regt

142. Prussia: von Malachowski's Hussars

143. Prussia: von Holstein's Infantry Regiment

144. Prussia: Pioneer battalions

145. Modena: Colonel's colour, Regg'to Reggio

146. Modena: battalion colour, Regg'to Reggio

PLATE 24

147. Britain: 1st guidon,
2nd Dragoon Guards

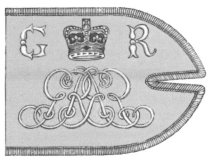

148. Britain: 3rd guidon,
2nd Dragoon Guards

149. Britain: King's colour,
9th Regt of Foot

150. Britain: Regimental colour,
2nd Queen's Regt

151. Austria: Sovereign's colour
for infantry (obverse)

152. Austria: Sovereign's colour
for infantry (reverse)

PLATE 25

153. England: King's Own Royal Regt

154. England: 3rd Regt of Foot

155. Scotland: Prince Charles Stuart's standard

156. Scotland: Lord Ogilvy's Regt

157. Scotland: Royal Écossais

PLATE 26

158. King's colour, 1st Royal Scots

159. Regimental colour, 1st Royal Scots

160. 27th Inniskilling Regt of Foot

161. 44th Regt of Foot

162. 55th Regt of Foot

163. 62nd Royal American Regt

PLATE 27

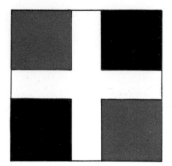

164. Régt de la Sarre

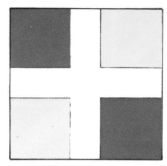

165. Régt de Guyenne

166. Régt de Berry

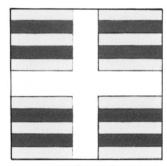

167. Régt de Béarn

168. Régt de Royal Roussillon

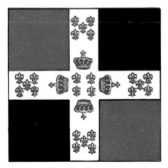

169. Régt de la Reine

PLATE 28

170. Prussia: Infantry Regt No. 1

171. Prussia: Infantry Regt No. 7

172. Prussia: Infantry Regt No. 4

173. Saxon artillery standard

174. Austria: regimental colour
for Austrian infantry

175. Austria: regimental colour
for Hungarian infantry

PLATE 29

176. Régt de Cosse Brissac

177. Régt de Saintonge

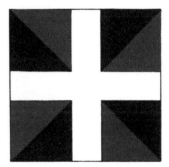

178. Régt de Briqueville

179. Régt de Limousin

180. Grenadiers de France

181. Régt de Royal Pologne

PLATE 30

182. Britain: 1st Foot Guards

183. Britain: 2nd Foot Guards

184. Russia: Garde à Cheval

185. Russia: 1st Regt of Grenadiers

186. Russia: line infantry pattern

187. Russia: Semenovski Life Guards

PLATE 31

188. Britain: 78th Highlanders, 1793

189. Britain: 86th Foot, 1807

190. Britain: 76th Foot, 1807

191. Britain: 19th Light Dragoons

192. French Corps in the service
of Tippoo Sahib

193. French infantry colour
(Gerrard?)

PLATE 32

194. Standard of Mysore

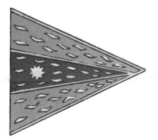

195. Standard of Mysore

196. Howdah banner
of Mysore

197. Gurkha colour

198. Bengali standard

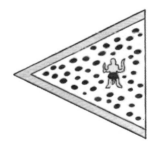

199. Bengali standard

200. East Indian standard

201. East Indian standard

PLATE 33

202. Poland: standard carried by irregulars

203. Poland: Krakow Grenadiers

204. Prussia: Infantry Regt No. 19

205. Prussia: Infantry Regt No. 15

206. Russia:
Novgorodski Cuirassier Regt

207. Russia:
Preobrajenski Life Guards

PLATE 34

208. King's colour, 9th Foot

209. Regimental colour, 9th Foot

210. 33rd Foot

211. 93rd Highlanders

212. 103rd Foot

213. King's colour, Queen's Rangers

PLATE 35

214. Brunswick: Regt von Rhetz

215. Brunswick: Regt von Specht

216. Hesse-Hanau: Erbprinz Regt

217. Anspach-Bayreuth Regts

218. Hesse-Cassel: Prinz Carl Regt

219. Hesse-Cassel: Leib du Corps

PLATE 36

220. Washington's Guard

221. Philadelphia Light Horse

222. 2nd Regt Light Dragoons

223. Webb's Continental Regt

224. 1st Continental Regt of Foot

225. Pulaski's Legion

PLATE 37

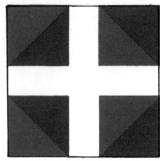

226. Régt de Gatinois

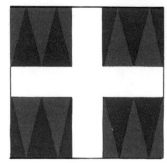

227. Régt de Hainault

228. Régt d'Agenois

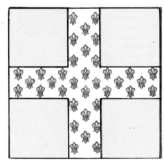

229. Artillerie du Roi

230. Walsh's Irish Regt

231. Royal Deux Ponts Régt

PLATE 38

232. Battalion colour, Walloon regts

233. Battalion colour, 1792-1804

234. Battalion colour, 1804-1806

235. Battalion colour, 1806-1816

236. Cavalry standard, 1792-1804

237. Cavalry standard, 1806-1816

PLATE 39

238. 1st Royals

239. Coldstream Guards

240. de Meuron's Swiss Regt

241. 23rd Light Dragoons

242. 3rd Battalion, 1st Foot Guards

243. 5th Battalion, King's German Legion

PLATE 40

244. Infantry colour, 1791-1794

245. Infantry colour, 1794-1804

246. 1804 eagle

247. Infantry colour, 1804

248. Infantry colour, 1812

249. Infantry colour, 1815

PLATE 41

250. Infantry Regt No. 3
(East Prussia)

251. Thuringia Hussar Regt

252. Dragoon Regt No. 26

253. Guard Cuirassier regiments

254. Dragoon Regt No. 3

255. Hanseatic Legion

PLATE 42

256. Foot Guards, 1796

257. Line infantry, 1800

258. Line infantry,
St George model, 1810

259. Dragoons, 1797 pattern

260. Cuirassier and
dragoon pattern, 1803

261. Banner of the Don Cossacks, 1803

PLATE 43

262. Baden: 2nd Infantry Regt

263. Bavarian infantry colour, 1803

264. Brunswick infantry colour, 1815

265. Nassau infantry colour, 1815

266. Saxon infantry colour, 1802-1811

267. Würzburg infantry colour

PLATE 44

268. Piedmont: Regg'to de Savoie

269. Cispadana Republic:
Lombard Legion

270. Naples: 1st Light Infantry

271. Naples: 7th Infantry

272. Kingdom of Italy:
Dragoni Della Regina

273. Kingdom of Italy:
3rd Regg'to Cacciatori a Cavallo

PLATE 45

274. Portugal: 11th Infantry Regt

275. Portugal: 21st Infantry Regt

276. Portugal:
7th Battalion of Caçadores

277. Spain: Battalion colour
Macarquibir Infantry Regt

278. Spain: Battalion colour
Irlanda Infantry Regt

279. Spain: artillery standard

PLATE 46

280. Polish Legion

281. Légion de la Vistule

282. 7th Infantry Regt

283. 13th Infantry Regt

284. 14th Infantry Regt

285. 15th Lancers

PLATE 47

286. France: Régt Irlandais

287. Holland: 5th Dutch Line

288. Sweden: Royal Swedois Regt

289. Switzerland: 3rd Demi Brigade
Auxiliaries Helvétiques

290. Army of Condé:
Grenadiers de Bourbon

291. Émigrés:
Régt des Dragons d'Enghien

PLATE 48

292. 7th Royal Fusiliers

293. 4th West India Regt

294. King's colour, 4th Foot

295. Regimental colour, 4th Foot

296. King's colour, Quebec Militia

297. Regimental colour, Quebec Militia

PLATE 49

298. 2nd Regt of Infantry

299. 4th Regt of Infantry

300. 68th James City Light Infantry

301. 1st Harford Light Dragoons

302. New York Militia

303. 1st Regt of Light Artillery

PLATE 50

304. General Miranda's flag

305. Argentina: General Belgrano's flag

306. Uruguay: Artigas' flag, 1815-20

307. Flag of the Andes Army, 1817-18

308. Peru: General San Martin's flag,
1820-22

309. Spain: Standard,
1821-1824

PLATE 51

310. Fr. Miguel Hidalgo's banner

311. Fr. José María Morelos' banner

312. General Iturbide's flag

313. Texan flag of 1835

314. New Orleans Greys

315. Newport Rifles, Kentucky

PLATE 52

316. Line infantry pattern

317. Kazanski Jaegers

318. Odesski Lancers

319. Akhtirski Hussars

320. Standard of the Host of Azov

321. 1st Regt of the
Host of the Black Sea

PLATE 53

322. Britain:
1st Battalion, Coldstream Guards

323. Britain: 4th Dragoon Guards

324. Britain: 55th Foot

325. Britain: 57th Foot

326. France: 67th Régt d'Infanterie

327. Sardinia: Royal Piedmont Regt

PLATE 54

328. Austria:
Sovereign's colour for infantry (obverse)

329. Austria:
Sovereign's colour for infantry (reverse)

330. Duchy of Parma:
1st Battalion of Infantry

331. Two Sicilies:
12th Regt of Infantry

332. Papal States:
Carabinieri Pontifici

333. Papal States:
Dragoni Pontifici

PLATE 55

334. National colour for infantry

335. Regimental standard for cavalry

336. Regimental standard for artillery

337. Artillery guidon

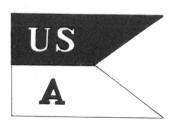

338. Cavalry guidon,
pre 1863 and post 1865

339. Cavalry guidon,
1863-65

PLATE 56

340. 23rd Corps

341. H.Q. flag, Army of the Potomac

342. Sheridan's guidon

343. Custer's guidon

344. 3rd Regt New Jersey Volunteers

345. 3rd Regt New Jersey Cavalry

PLATE 57

346. 1st National flag

347. 2nd National flag

348. 3rd National flag

349. Battle flag

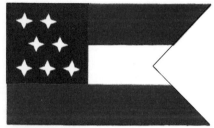

350. Cavalry guidon

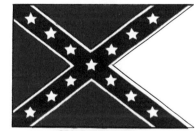

351. Cavalry guidon

352. Stuart's Horse Artillery

353. Washington Artillery

PLATE 58

354. South Carolina: State colour

355. South Carolina: State colour

356. North Carolina: State colour

357. Florida: Independent Blues Company

358. Texas: State colour

359. Texas: 'Bonnie Blue Flag'

360. Louisiana: State colour

361. Virginia, State colour

PLATE 59

362. Austria:
Sovereign's standard for cavalry

363. Prussia:
Guard Grenadier regiments

364. Prussia:
Battalion colour, line infantry regts

365. Prussia:
standard for line cavalry

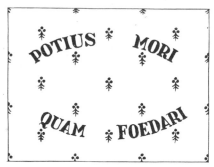

366. France: Breton seamen's flag

367. France: Alsatian irregulars

PLATE 60

368. Germany:
3rd Battalion Marine Infantry

369. Germany:
Bavarian infantry colour

370. Germany:
91st (Oldenburg) Infantry Regt

371. Russia: Sevski Regt

372. Russia: Kostromski Regt

373. Russia: Army of the Urals
(Cossacks)

PLATE 61

374. Standard of the Bey of Tunisia

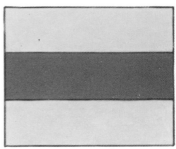

375. Tunisian flag

376. Chinese
general's
pennant

377. Sudanese standard

378. Standard of
King Behazin of Dahomey

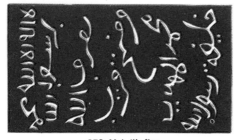

379. Mahdi's flag

380. Free Corps
of Krügersdorf, Transvaal

PLATE 62

381. Queen's colour,
106th Bombay Light Infantry

382. Regimental colour,
106th Bombay Light Infantry

383. 27th Bombay Light Infantry

384. 108th Madras Infantry

385. 2nd Punjab Infantry

386. 1st Lancers, Hyderabad Contingent

PLATE 63

387. Britain:
73rd Highlanders

388. Britain:
1st Battalion, Grenadier Guards

389. Britain:
27th Inniskilling Regt

390. Britain:
1st Battalion,
23rd Royal Welch Fusiliers

391. South Africa:
Weatherley's Horse

392. South Africa:
Uitenhage Volunteer Rifles

PLATE 64

PLATE DESCRIPTIONS

THIRTY YEARS WAR 1618–1648

1. Bavaria: von Tilly's Dragoons

In the early seventeenth century the Hapsburg Emperor ruled a network of semi-independent states stretching from the Rhine to Poland and from the Danish border to the edge of the Ottoman Empire. At this time there was no Imperial standing army and the Emperor drew his forces from his hereditary lands of Austria and Hungary, being dependent for the remainder of his forces on the German princes. Therefore, at the outbreak of war in 1618 the Emperor borrowed 25,000 mercenaries under Count von Tilly from Bavaria and the Catholic League.

The guidon of Johan Tserclaes von Tilly's Dragoon Company is the oldest-known dragoon guidon in existence, having been made before 1609 for von Tilly's Dragoons, formed by Archduke Matthias from a Walloon infantry regiment originally raised in 1603. Dragoons were introduced during the latter part of the sixteenth tury and their guidons were initially diminutive versions of the swallow-tailed cavalry pennons of that century. Later they were to develop their own identity, following more closely the infantry colours, as befitted mounted infantry. The reverse of this guidon bore the Archduke's monogram surrounded by a laurel wreath and under an archducal crown. The abbreviated slogan shown means St Michael Pray for Us.

Size: Length 157 cm (68 cm to the fork). Breadth 78 cm.

2. Friedland-Mecklenburg: Wallenstein's Life Regt

In 1625 a private army raised by Albrecht von Wallenstein, Duke of Friedland and Mecklenburg, was added to the forces of the Emperor and from then on Wallenstein commanded the Hapsburg armies. Wallenstein's army appears to have been more uniformly dressed than Tilly's, and some regiments had flags in the colours of their coats. Thus Berchtold von Waldstein's regiment had green flags, Maximilian von Waldstein's yellow flags. Balkan irregulars carried large triangular flags. The colour illustrated was made in the latter part of the 1620s and is attributed to one of the companies of Wallenstein's Household Regiment, which was absorbed into Julius Hardegg's Regiment in 1629. Colours with borders are characteristic of the armies of Austria, Bavaria and Spain: such borders are not found on the colours of Protestant countries at this date. The extremely large size is an inheritance from the Renaissance, and flags in general became smaller as the century progressed.

93

Size: Length 384 cm. Breadth 311 cm.

3. Archduke Leopold's guidon

During the Thirty Years War army commanders had their own guidons as symbols of command. The example shown is probably the most famous of its type, the personal guidon of the Imperial commander-in-chief, Archduke Leopold Wilhelm, captured at Leipzig in 1642. On the reverse is Christ's cross and the inscription TIMORE DOMINI, with a lion and lamb at the foot of the cross.

Ferdinand II, Emperor 1619–37, was noted for his piety and many flags carried during his reign bore religious figures such as the one illustrated here. However, during his reign was instigated a system, possibly copied from the French army, whereby the premier company of a regiment carried a white silk *Leibfahne* or Sovereign's colour, while the other companies carried colours bearing the Imperial eagle, a shield on its breast displaying Ferdinand's arms. This system of a distinctive colonel's colour and a basic pattern for the colours of other companies was adopted in the middle years of the war and was at first limited to regiments in the employ of the Emperor, but gradually spread until it was used by most of the countries involved in the war.

4. Hessian cavalry standard

Made in 1631 for a cavalry company raised by the abbot of Fulda, this standard was captured in the same year at Vacha. The reverse is shown here: the black field from the abbey's arms (a black cross), the three lilies of Fulda's arms on the shield and banner of St Simplicius. On the obverse is shown St Boniface, patron saint of Fulda Abbey.

Size: Length 58 cm. Breadth 53 cm.

5. Saxony: Starschadel Infantry Regt

The company colour illustrated dates from 1633 and it is known that by this date the colonel's company of the regiment was carrying a white colour. The motto *Absque Metu* may also have appeared on both Leibfahne and company colours: it is not shown on the source consulted.

6. Brunswick cavalry standard

Made in 1632 for the Red Regiment of Horse commanded by Colonel von Mützephal, this standard was captured at Gröbzig four years later. The inscription (I will crush them) and the devices on the standard symbolize the Protestant duchy's war against Catholicism. The obverse bears the crowned monogram FV for Duke Frederick Ulrich of Brunswick Wolfenbüttel, brother in law to Gustavus Adolphus.

Size: Length 56 cm. Breadth 51 cm.

7. Bavaria: von Tilly's Infantry Regt

The Virgin Mary was the patroness of Bavaria and her image was therefore used for the colonel's colour, as in many other Catholic countries. The colour shown is a company colour of

Werner von Tilly's Regiment, made between 1620 and 1630 and captured by the Swedes at Rinteln in 1633. Like the Austrian colours of this date, it has a multi-coloured border: blue and white from the arms of Bavaria; black and gold from those of the Palatinate. On the reverse the religious text reads DOMINA SANCTA MARIA SAL-VVM FAC IMPERATOREM NOSTRVM ET EXAVDI NOS IN DIE QVA INVOCAVERI-NIVS TE.

Size: Length 283 cm. Breadth 259 cm.

8. Bavarian dragoon guidon
This guidon was captured by the Swedes sometime between 1630 and 1647. The obverse shows Christ on the cross with the texts JESVS NASARENVS REX IVDEORVM: TITVLVS TRIVMPHALIS. AB OMNIBVS ME DEFENDAT MALIS. IN HOC SIGNO VINCES.

Size: Length 227 cm (121 cm to fork). Breadth 111 cm.

9. Bavarian cavalry standard
This standard, in the colours of the Bavarian arms, was made between 1630 and 1647 and bears the cypher sDMsVBs. On the reverse the Virgin Mary is portrayed in the Annunciation.

Size: Length 45 cm. Breadth 52 cm.

10. Elector of Bavaria's standard
Captured by the Swedes in 1646, this cavalry standard of Ferdinand of Bavaria bears on its reverse the arms of Ferdinand as Elector of Cologne, flanked by two saints.

11. Spanish cavalry standard
The standard was made sometime between 1630 and the end of the war. The monogram CYL stands for Castile and Leon: the inscription means 'I understand'. Other patterns for Spanish cavalry standards included religious subjects and texts, with the emphasis on portraits of the Holy Virgin.

Size: 47 cm square – smaller than most cavalry standards of this period.

12. Spanish infantry colour
The kingdom of Spain was inherited by Charles V in 1516 and became part of the Hapsburg Empire: the cross of Burgundy (or cross raguly in heraldic terms) was therefore inaugurated on Spanish colours and standards from this date. The early seventeenth-century example illustrated shows a common form of parti-coloured field. Other colours of this type were in blue/white and black/white. Green/white chequered fields were also used, as were plain white fields, but these colours usually had a border, often of green and white diagonal stripes.

Size: all these infantry colours were in the region of 180 cm square.

13–16. Swedish colours and cornet
There is little information available on Swedish military flags prior to the mid-seventeenth century and the majority of flags which survive from the Thirty Years War era are those of foreign regiments in the Swedish service. However, the main emblems

95

occurring on these are the Swedish arms (**14**) or the monogram of the king (**34**), and it is safe to assume these emblems were common to the Swedish regiments also. Gustavus Adolphus' regiments also appear to have carried flags in the colour of their brigade – the brigades being named after the flag colours, *not* coat colours – and there does not seem to have been any link between uniform and flag colour as existed in Wallenstein's army. Some of the brigades were Black, Blue and Yellow (German regiments); Green (mainly Scots); and White and Red.

13 illustrates a typical colour of the period, that of Robert Monroe's infantry regiment, *circa* 1630. The reverse was identical except the key on the shield was replaced by a crowned lion rampant in gold.

Johan Banér's Life Regiment's colour (**14**) *circa* 1630 is also typical, bearing as it does the quartered arms of Sweden (three gold crowns) and Gothland, with the arms of the king (the golden wheatsheaf of the House of Vasa) in the centre. A white colour, possibly the *Livfana* or Colonel's colour, of a similar pattern was also carried by this regiment. Differences were DEO ET VICTRICIBVS ARMIS along the top in gold; a gold flaming grenade in each of the bottom corners, pointing towards the centre; the shield and crown in the centre surrounded by a continuous wreath and with a hand coming from the top left to rest on the crown.

Banér's Regiment also had a cavalry cornet (**15**), the reverse of which bore the cypher GAKVS topped by a crown, all in gold. **16** illustrates one

of the colours carried by Johan Forbes' Regiment *circa* 1630. GARS (Gustavus Adolphus Rex Sueclae) was the usual cypher of the king at this time.

17. Danish cavalry standard

Until 1664 it was customary in Denmark for the standards and colours of the various divisions within a regiment to be decorated with different parts of the Danish coat of arms, while the *Dannebrog* (red cross on a white field) was carried in the canton. The standard illustrated, made at Viborg in 1648 for a company of the new Jutland cavalry, bears the Norwegian coat of arms as its distinction.

Size: Length 65 cm. Breadth 54 cm.

18. Denmark: Frederick III's Infantry Regt

This colour belonged to a company of the regiment commanded by Frederick (later Frederick III of Denmark), in his capacity of Archbishop of Bremen, sometime between 1635-45. Its large size and the allegorical picture are typical of many infantry colours employed by Protestant countries until the fashion changed about 1635. The national colours in the Dannebrog are reversed, possibly for the younger branch of the Royal House, to which Frederick then belonged. The mottoes read: DOMINUS PROVIDEBIT/GUTE BEDACHTSAMBKEIT MÄNNLICHE TAPFFERKEIT/GEHÖREN BEIDE ZUM STREIT. And in the centre: CUI VULT.

Size: Length 266 cm. Breadth 207 cm.

19. Saxon cavalry standard
The persistence into the seventeenth century of the knight's banner and his attitude to war are aptly illustrated by the Saxon cavalry standards of this period. The one illustrated, dated about 1635–45, indicates that the knight should be satisfied by forcing his foe to the ground and should then treat him honourably. The slogan reads 'To Pass is Sufficient'. This example is also typical of the small square or squarish standards which began to replace the large pointed standards of the medieval and Renaissance periods in Western Europe during the first decades of the seventeenth century.

Size: Length 53 cm. Breadth 52 cm.

20. Saxony: Franz Albrecht's Regiment
A standard carried by one of the troops of the regiment raised by Franz Albrecht of Saxony-Lauenburg, *circa* 1690, and commanded by Colonel Trauditsch.

21–25. French infantry colours
During the Wars of Religion (1562–98) the Huguenot party adopted a white flag and when in 1589 the Protestant Henry IV became the first Bourbon king of France, the white flag became the premier flag of the kingdom and its army. The white cross of the French crusaders had been used on French army flags since Louis XI organized the first national infantry bands in 1479, and it was natural therefore that the white cross should be perpetuated in the flags of

the new army which Henry IV created in 1597 by making the Picardy, Champagne, Navarre and Piedmont 'Regiments' permanent formations, along with the Gardes Françaises (**139**). The colonel's colour of these regiments was therefore a white cross with golden fleurs-de-lis on a white field, cross and field almost indistinguishable because even the stitching was white. Elite regiments, such as the Guards, usually added a special device. The other colours of the regiment, one per company, were known as *drapeaux d'ordonnance* and were of simple design – the white cross with the four parts of the quartered field in the colours assigned to the regiments. Picardy (**21**), Navarre (**22**) and Champagne (**23**) are illustrated: Piedmont had a black field. These permanent regiments were joined in the early seventeenth century by the Régiment d'Auvergne (**24**), raised in 1606, which used a more complicated combination of colours; the Régiment de Normandie (yellow field); and the Régiment de la Marine (**25**), formed in 1627. This simple yet effective system of differentiating between the flags of regiments remained in use until the Revolution at the end of the eighteenth century.

Size: in excess of 180 cm square.

26. France: Les Gardes Écossaises
Les Gardes Écossaises were raised in 1633 for the French service and distinguished themselves at Rocroi in 1643, where the colour illustrated was carried. There does not appear to have been lettering on the scroll.

The regiment was used to augment the Scots Company of the Garde du Corps, which under Louis XIII (1610–43) carried the white standard of the Bourbons but with the device of a running greyhound in a field surrounded by trees and the motto IN OMNI MODO FIDELIS.

POLISH WARS 1600–1677

27. Polish guidon

The wheatsheaf of the House of Vasa on the white eagle of Poland dates this guidon at sometime between 1587 and 1660. Its large size is typical of the large swallow-tailed pennons used in Western Europe in the sixteenth century. These were replaced during the early seventeenth century by smaller ones, often square, and this guidon probably belongs to this period. However, the larger pennons continued to be used in Eastern Europe during the remainder of the seventeenth century. The border bears the Polish *gozdawa* coat of arms, a double lily.

Size: Length 313 cm (176 cm to the fork). Breadth 160 cm.

28. King of Poland's Household Troops

Made sometime between 1632 and 1660, this standard is of considerable size and the high quality of its ornamentation suggests it belonged to a troop of Life Guards or others of the king's household cavalry. The coat of arms, composed of the Polish and Swedish arms, is interesting in that it shows the idea of a union between Poland and Sweden had survived the death of Sigismund in 1632. The obverse bears a cross with the Virgin and Child in its centre, standing on a crescent moon and surrounded by a halo of sunbeams. At the top is PRO GLORIA CRUCIS, at the bottom SUB TUO PRAESIDIO.

Size: Length 78 cm. Breadth 99 cm.

29. Polish cavalry standard

It is difficult to categorize this flag as it is guidon shaped but the size of an infantry colour. Because of this and its design it is perhaps best to call it a standard, in the medieval sense. It was made sometime between the end of the sixteenth century and 1660. The arms are probably those of the captain who raised the company, and the flag is therefore a late example of the medieval heraldic 'banner' on which the coat of arms was the only insignia. Banners with a round cut fly were frequently used during the sixteenth century and it is probable this standard dates from the turn of the century rather than mid-seventeenth century.

Size: Length 240 cm. Breadth 148 cm.

30. Cavalry guidon of Tartars in Polish service

The Poles made use of Tartar auxiliaries during the First Northern War
and the guidon illustrated was cap
tured from those auxiliaries by the
Swedes. The Arabic means 'There is
no god but Allah, and Mohammed is
the Prophet of Allah.'

31-34. Swedish colours and standards

The flags illustrated here show that in
the first half of the seventeenth century Swedish military flags were still
in a transitional stage between the
large Renaissance flags and the bar-
oque style of regulated flags of the
later seventeenth century. The colour
of von Liebenstein's German Regiment in the Swedish service (31), *circa*
1630, is typical of the type referred
to by Swedish authorities as Lands-
knecht. The standard of Magnus de
la Gardie's Life Regiment (32), *circa*
1650, bears the monogram MDLG and
is presumably his personal standard,
and likewise the standard of Carl
Gustaf's Life Regiment (33), dating
from 1656, appears to bear a personal
emblem. The reverse of this standard
is shown in 57. However, by 1672, the
date of the *Livfana* of Carl XI's German Guard (34), Swedish flags were
conforming to an established system.
(The surviving flag shows only two
crowns as illustrated, but part of the
flag is missing and there were probably four crowns, one in each corner.)
The type of colour carried by the
other companies of this regiment is
shown in 75.

35. Russia: Czar Alexis Michailo-vitch's Regt

The cavalry standards of the Czar's
Life Guards were changed from the
earlier pennon type to a square form
during the latter part of the reign of
Michael Fedorovitch (1613–45). This
particular standard was made between 1645–56 and was probably
captured in 1656 during the siege of
Riga. The reverse bears the Cross of
Christ. The main device of St Eusta-
thius on horseback was used in 1664
on the standard of the second company of the Czar's own regiment.

36. Russia: Czar's standard

The first standard of a Russian regiment at this date was known as the
Czar's standard. The one illustrated
was probably made in 1654 for the
approaching war with Poland and
was captured by the Poles near Smolensk on 5 July 1654. The Swedes
took the standard from the Poles in
Warsaw the following year. This
single-tongued form of 'standard',
originating in the medieval pennon,
was fairly common in Russia until
about 1700.
Size: Length 485 cm (140 cm to the
'fork'). Breadth 160 cm.

37. Russia: 12th Regt Streltzi of Moscow

The fourteen regiments of Moscow
Streltzi (sharpshooters) had served in
the Kremlin since 1555 and 2000 of
the men formed a Life Guard for the
Czar. All carried a colour of the basic
design illustrated, though most bore
no emblems and had plain borders,

Regiment	Field	Cross	Corners	Border
1st	Raspberry	White	—	—
2nd	Grey	Raspberry	—	Yellow
3rd	Bright green	Raspberry	—	White
4th	Red	Yellow	Yellow	White
5th	Red	Yellow	Bright blue	White
6th	Yellow	Dark raspberry	White	Bright green
7th	Bright blue	Yellow	Yellow	Black
8th	Orange	White	—	Green

sometimes with squares of a different colour at each corner.

38. Russian banner of 1645–76 era
This is a typical example of the banners carried in this period by the

Fig. 2

smaller units of the Russian army. Others of this type portrayed different saints and were in different col-ours. The reverse had the same border but bore in the centre the Russian 'saint's cross' (fig. 2) flanked by a lance and another shaft topped by a sponge, all standing on five steps.

Size: approximately 150 cm square.

Turkish standards (not illustrated) Turkish forces were commanded by their local governors who were of various ranks and usually carried some form of standard rather than flag; all the high-ranking command-ers for example had horse-hair stand-ards. The Sultan had a horse-hair standard of seven tails; a Grand Vizier or army commander a standard of four tails; a *Beglar-Beg* (or *Beyler-bey*), governor of a *Vilayet* or province, a standard with one tail. *Sanjak-begs*, governors of a *Sanjak* or sub-division of a *Vilayet*, had a flag surmounted by a gilt ball. The horse tails were white, decorated with red and blue ribbons, and were carried on red staves topped by gilt balls, though the individual tails might be surmounted by cres-cents.

These wars saw the use of many types of flags, with every company of infantry and every troop of cavalry having its own flag, as was the custom in Europe. As early as 1622 'rules' had been published in England governing the use of infantry colours (see Historical Background) and from the beginning of the war the infantry colours of both sides followed a system whereby the regiment was identified by a colour, sometimes but not always the colour of the regiment's coats, and the individual companies by symbols, usually taken from the arms or the badge of the colonel. Both sides also claimed the cross of St George as their symbol. Infantry colours therefore bore a canton for England, a colour for the regiment and a device for the company. This regularization of colours was confirmed when the New Model Army was organized in 1645.

Size: approximately 195 cm square.

In the cavalry the captains raised their own troops and displayed on their standards such devices as they thought proper: heraldic symbols and mottoes, quotations and allegorical figures or scenes were freely used for their propaganda value, in the same style as the flags of the Thirty Years War. After the first year of war some degree of standardization began to emerge, following the example of the infantry, and the colonel's troop often carried a plain standard of a chosen colour, the other troops of the regiment using standards of the same colour but each troop having a distinctive device. However, the choice of device was still very much in the captain's hands, and there was little similarity between troops. Dragoons, being mounted infantry, followed the system employed by the infantry, except their flags were guidon-shaped.

39–44. Royalist colours and standards

Colonel Leveson's Regiment of Horse (**39**) had two other standards: 1) Sable, an ostrich Or, holding in its mouth a sword proper, and standing on a scroll with the motto HOC NU-TRIOR. 2) A scroll with the letters s.a.–s.a. The King's Life Guard of Foot (**41**) had five other standards, including: 1) Argent, the cross of St George, impaling Gules, a rose Or, seeded Gules and surmounted by a royal crown Or. 2) The same, impaling two roses in pale, each surmounted by a crown. 3) The same, impaling Gules, a griffin rampant Or.

Colonel Bagott raised a regiment of Foot (**43**) and another of Horse. The latter carried three blue standards without any badge, motto or other distinction. Colonel Taylor's Regiment of Foot (**44**), from Bristol, had six colours of which two are recorded, that illustrated and another similar but with the addition of another heart in bend.

Montrose's personal flag in the 1650 campaign was white, bearing a lion about to leap across a river running between two rocks, and the motto NIL MEDIUM. His Horse regiments carried black standards bearing three pairs of clasped hands holding swords, and the motto QUOS PIETAS VIRTUS ET HONOR FECIT AMICOS. The Foot regiments also had black flags bearing the severed head of Charles I and the motto DEO ET VICTRICIBUS ARMIS.

45–50. London Trained Bands

The colonel's colour of the Tower Hamlets Regiment (45) is an exception to the regularized method outlined above, bearing as it does a slogan and design similar to the type carried on earlier colours. The Lt-Col.'s colour was similar but with the cross of St George in the canton, as 46: the Major's as the Lt-Col.'s but with one silver roundel next to the canton. The 1st Captain's colour had two roundels, 2nd Captain's three, and 3rd Captain's four. These roundels were borne in a straight line along the top of the colour.

Colonel's colours were normally plain and this was the case for all other regiments listed here. The Lt-Col.'s colour for all these regiments had the St George's canton added, the Major's as the Lt-Col.'s but with the addition of one of the regiment's insignia. In the case of the Orange Regiment (46) this was a white trefoil. The captains' colours were as the Major's but with two insignia for the 1st Captain, three for the 2nd Captain etc. The Orange Regiment appears to have had only three captains, whose trefoils were placed diagonally as in 48.

The White Regiment (47) had four captains. The lozenges of the 1st and 2nd Captains were placed diagonally, but those of the 3rd formed a square

and those of the 4th were as in 50. The Green and Blue Regiments (48 and 49) each had three captains, and their devices were placed diagonally on all colours. The Yellow Regiment (50) had four captains, the first three bearing their stars diagonally, the 4th Captain having his five stars placed as illustrated.

51–56. Parliamentarian standards and guidon

Hundreds of individual standards were recorded at the time of the wars and it is possible to only illustrate a few typical examples here. However, colonel's standards, being usually plain, can be conveniently listed. For example, Sir Edward Hartham of Leicestershire and Captains Berry, Thomson, Likcott, Neal and Mason all carried a plain red standard with a red and white border as in 56. Colonel Goodwin carried a plain red standard with a white border. Captain Dobbins of Worcestershire and Captain Gold carried red standards with red and gold borders. All these standards were square and considerably smaller than the infantry colours.

The dragoon guidon (54) shows how the dragoons followed the infantry pattern. The 3rd Regiment appears to have had four captains, the fourth captain bearing five roundels. The roundels were arranged thus:

. .. .·. :: .·.

The Scottish infantry fighting for Parliament made great use of numerals on their colours for identifying the companies and all bore the cross of St Andrew.

57–58. Swedish colours and standards

Sometime during Carl X's reign (1654–60) the trend towards a white colonel's colour and various coloured flags for the other companies within a regiment, which had begun in the second half of the Thirty Years War, was formalized into a regular system, with a white colonel's colour bearing the Swedish arms or king's monogram, and the company colours in provincial colours with devices chosen by the colonel.

The standard illustrated by **57** is dated 1658 and belongs to the Life Regiment of Carl X: the obverse of this standard is shown in **33**. **58** shows the colonel's guidon of a dragoon regiment at about the same date. Both bear Carl X's cypher, C.G.R.S., Carl Gustavus Rex Sueclae.

59. Poland: John Casimir's standard

During the winter of 1655–6 John Casimir returned to Poland to lead the Polish National Resistance against the Swedes and in the spring drove Carl back into Prussia. The standard illustrated was probably made in 1655 and was used by Casimir during the war of 1655–60. It bears the wheat-sheaf emblem of Vasa, to which house Casimir belonged.

60. Polish cavalry pennon

This pennon was captured by the Swedes sometime before the peace of 1660. The image of God's right arm bearing a sword was frequently used during the sixteenth and seventeenth centuries but in Poland it specifically signified the king.

Size: Length 101 cm. Breadth 55 cm.

61. Russian banner of 1645–76 era

A typical banner of the reign of Czar Alexis Michailovitch (1645–76). The figure in the centre is Constantine the Great.

Size: 150 cm square.

62. Denmark: Jörgen Rosenkrantz's Regiment

This infantry colour was made at Hamburg in 1657 for a company of Rosenkrantz's regiment and bears as its device the goddess Fortuna. The colonel's colour would have been white, as was now the custom; the colours of the other companies blue with other allegorical motifs.

Size: Length 212 cm. Breadth 207 cm.

63. France: Régiment du Roi

This regiment was formed in 1665 and carried the *drapeau d'ordonnance* illustrated from then until 1669 (see also **118**). The colour is of the type described under **21–25**, but bears the fleur-de-lis of France to indicate it is an elite regiment. French colours were carried on staves three metres long, with a gilt finial 30 cm high and in the shape of a fleur-de-lis. A white cravat, 235 cm long and with gold fringes at the ends, was looped round the stave just below the finial. These details were the same for all infantry colours throughout the pre-revolution period.

Size: circa 180 cm square.

64. France: Régiment de Carignan

The regiment was raised by Thomas Francis of Savoy, Prince of Carignan, and by 1667 had served France for some twenty-five years. In 1664 the regiment was ordered to Canada to subdue the Iroquois and Henri de Chapelas, Sieur de Salières, one of the most outstanding captains, was given command of the regiment. Its name was then changed to Carignan-Salières. Most of the members of the regiment returned to France in 1667 and were absorbed into the Régiment de Lorraine, which probably had colours with a field of grey (1 and 4) and violet with green dots (2 and 3). Contrary to custom Carignan took only the white colonel's colour to America,

but regiments sent to America later also took their *drapeau d'ordonnance.*

Size: circa 180 cm square.

65–66. Britain: King's and Queen's Troops, Horse Guards

The Life Guard of Horse was raised in 1661 as a personal guard for the king and originally consisted of three troops, His Majesty's Own, Queen's and Duke of Albemarle's. Each troop had a standard and a guidon, the latter of the same design as the standards illustrated but rounded and split at the fly. The standard of the third troop was as for the King's Troop but with a scalloped border of black silk cord. In 1670 the Duke died, 3rd Troop became the 2nd Queen's and the 2nd became the 3rd Duke of York's. In 1684 the 3rd Troop carried a yellow standard and guidon, bearing the Duke's cypher and coronet.

Size: about 240 cm square.

67–68. Swedish standards

Illustrated are the standard of the Viborg Cavalry Regiment (**68**) dating from 1665, and a dragoon 'guidon' (**67**), which in fact takes the form of a standard, of the same period. Both bear the cypher of Carl XI (1660–97). The Viborg Cavalry Regiment also carried a green standard bearing a knight charging on a grey horse, the date 1666, and slogans in German.

69. France: Colonel-General of Dragoons

In 1668 a colonel-general (Lauzun) was appointed to command the corps of dragoons. The colonel-general and the corps were represented by a single white guidon bearing the corner cyphers as illustrated and carried by the first company of the colonel-general's regiment. Other companies carried the coloured guidon as illustrated.

club and lion skin and the motto IN-FRACTU FRANGIT: a second standard as the first but the field red. The Royal regiments had blue standards bearing the golden ornaments as Fig. 3; the reverse bearing a semée of gold fleur-de-lis. The reverse was the same for the Royal Navarre, Royal Normandie, Royal Champagne, Royal Picardie and Royal Lorraine Regiments but the obverse was charged

Fig. 3

The cravat was as for the infantry but shorter, and the finial took the form of a simple spearhead.

70. France: Dragons d'Orléans

From 1635 French cavalry carried the following standards: the regiment of the colonel-general, a white standard with gold ornaments as illustrated by Fig. 3, with on the reverse Hercules'

with the arms of the province surmounted by a royal crown. White appears on the standards of only two regiments: Chartres, obverse crimson, semée of gold fleur-de-lis and in the centre the arms of Orléans; reverse white, semée of the arms of Orléans. Bourgogne, obverse blue with a gold fleur-de-lis in each corner, in the centre a phoenix rising from flames; reverse, white and bearing the red cross raguly of Burgundy. Dragoon guidons followed this basic design, as illustrated by the guidon of the Dragons d'Orléans.

71. France: Cent-Suisses de la Garde

The Cent-Suisses was established by Charles VIII in 1496 and was the first permanent Swiss unit outside Switzerland. The colour illustrated was issued in 1616 and carried until 1669. The later version had EA EST on the horizontal arms and GENTIS on the fourth arm of the cross, a coat of arms at the centre of the cross, and the 1st and 4th quarters had the cypher replaced by another gold rod, the three then bound by a red ribbon, the whole bordered by gold fleur-de-lis.

72. France: Régiment de la Couronne

Battle honours as we know them did not exist on colours and standards prior to the French Revolution but there is a single exception in the French Royal Army – a Latin inscription on the colours of the Régiment de la Couronne. Raised in 1643 as the Régiment d'Artois, this regiment received its new name from Louis XIV for bravery at the siege of Maestricht in 1673 and was granted the privilege of a royal regiment (a blue field) and the right to bear a crown on its colours. The inscription DEDIT HANC MASTREKA CORONAM (Maestricht was the reason for this crown) is shown on the regiment's colours of 1747 but it is not known if it was used before that date. The crown was carried on the colours from 1673, when new colours were issued to the regiment.

Size: in excess of 180 cm square.

73. French or Bavarian infantry colour

This colour was captured by the Swedes before the peace of 1679. Its country of origin cannot be positively identified for the arms in the bottom corners were borne by thirty European families while the combination of blue and white was used not only by Bavaria but also by France. The emblem of a sword from heaven was used by Henry IV of France (died 1610) but was also used by many other countries in the seventeenth century. Only the fact that it does not follow the recognized pattern for French military flags leads one to suppose it might be Bavarian.

Size: Length 203 cm. Breadth 167 cm.

74. Britain: King's Own Royal Regiment of Dragoons

This regiment, commanded by John Churchill, was present at the battle of Enzheim on 4 October 1674. Its guidons were crimson with the following devices: Colonel, the royal cypher and crown; Lt-Col. as illustrated; 1st Troop, top of a beacon crowned Or with flames proper; 2nd Troop, two ostrich feathers crossed saltire-wise and a crown in silver; 3rd Troop, a rose and pomegranate impaled, leaves and stalk Vert; 4th Troop, a phoenix rising from flames.

Size: (probably) Length 75 cm. Breadth 67·5 cm.

75. Sweden: His Majesty's German Guard

The regimental or *övrigfana* of the German Guard in 1672. The Sovereign's colour or *Livfana* for this regiment at this date is shown in 34. Note the cypher now used by Carl XI in place of the CRS used earlier.

76. Sweden: August of Saxe-Halle's Infantry Regt

Probably the colonel's colour of 1678. The fly of the original in Copenhagen is missing and the motto DEO REGI ET GREGI is an assumption based on the surviving ET GREGI. This design was used continuously from the early seventeenth century onwards by Swedish regiments.

77. King of Denmark's Bodyguard

The Life Guard Regiment of the Danish Guards was founded by Frederick III in 1658 as the Horse Guards and was changed to the Regiment of Foot Guards in 1684. The regiment fought as mercenaries on the side of England's William of Orange against James II (War of League of Augsburg, 1692) and again under Marlborough during the war of the Spanish Succession, 1701–13. The colonel's colour was of white silk.

78. Strasbourg mounted burgher company

Strasbourg remained neutral in the Third Dutch War but in September 1674 was seized by the allies and over the next three years was the scene of much bitter fighting. The standard shown was carried by a burgher company from 1665 until 1681, when Louis XIV annexed the city.

79. Brandenburg: Duke Ernst Bogislav Croy's Cavalry Regt

This standard was probably made in 1677 for Croy's Cavalry Regiment, commanded by Colonel von Hülsen, and was captured by the Swedes on the island of Rügen the following year. The arms are those of the Elector Frederick William of Brandenburg, reading from top left: 1) Brandenburg, red eagle on silver; 2) Julich, black lion on gold; 3) Cleves, eight gold lily stems and silver shield on red; 4) Prussia, black eagle on silver; 5) the Electorship, gold sceptre on blue, crowned by Elector's cap; 6) Berg, red lion on gold; 7) Stettin, red griffin on blue; 8) Pomerania, red griffin on silver; 9) Hohenzollern, quartered shield of black and silver. The two wild men are the supporters of the Brandenburg arms.

Size: Length 55 cm. Breadth 53 cm.

80. Brandenburg: Simon von Bolsey's Marines

This captain's colour was made in the Netherlands in 1675 for a company of Bolsey's marines, which were enlisted in that country. Two other company colours and a white colonel's colour for this regiment, all bearing the same devices as illustrated, have also survived. The sceptre and red cap are symbols of the Brandenburg Electorship, while the orange twigs with fruits indicate the country of origin.

Size: Length 203 cm. Breadth 205 cm.

81. Sweden: H.M. Life Guards
Colonel's standard dating from 1686 and bearing the cypher, crown and lions used on the Guards' colours since at least 1672. (See **34**.) The semée of smaller crowns may be to indicate the regiment is an elite one. The standard is listed as such, not as a colour, and this would seem to indicate that by the last quarter of the century the cavalry was following the same patterns as the infantry.

82. Sweden: Västmanland company of the Life Regt
Sovereign's standard of the Västmanland Company of Carl XI's Livregemente, dating from 1686. The reverse has the same border and crown but a double c cypher under the crown, the whole flanked by palm branches.

83–84. Sweden: H.M. German Life Regt
Livfana and *övrigfana* of His Majesty's Tyska Livregemente in 1686. By this date it appears to have been common practice to use the two different cyphers on the two colours.

85. Sweden: Västgöta Cavalry Regt
Standard of the Västergötland Cavalry Regiment in 1686. The regiment had a second standard with the same field but bearing a rampant lion, gold in the black part, black in the gold part, and with a gold six-pointed star each side of the lion on the diagonal dividing line. Other squadrons carried standards bearing these devices but on a field divided by two diagonal lines into four triangles, the hoist and fly triangles being black, those at top and foot being gold. The Östergötland Cavalry Regiment had a standard similar to that illustrated but on a black field, and a second standard bearing a gold griffin rampant, again on a black field.

86. Sweden: Närke-Värmlands Infantry Regt
Colour carried by this regiment in 1686. The Östgöta Infantry Regiment carried a colour of similar colours and design but bearing a crowned griffin rampant in gold in place of the crossed arrows and without the four roses.

87. France: Régiment de Bourgogne
This regiment was raised in 1667 but did not follow the national pattern, using the cross raguly of Burgundy on a white field of fleur-de-lis instead. The Royal Comtois Regiment, formed in 1674, was the only other regiment to carry this pattern; a red cross raguly on an orange field, semée of gold fleur-de-lis.
Size: in excess of 180 cm square.

88. France: Régiment de Bretagne
The colonel's colour follows the basic pattern for infantry colours but the cross bears the ermine of Brittany. The company colours were black (1 and 4) and orange (2 and 3) and may have borne the motto one word to each arm of the cross.
Size: in excess of 180 cm square.

89. France: Les Gardes Suisses
The regiment of Swiss Guards was raised in 1616 by Louis XIII to augment the Cent-Suisses. The colonel's colour is illustrated; on the *drapeaux d'ordonnance* the 'rays' were of red and yellow alternately. Colours of these types were carried by the regiment within the French Royal Army until 1792.
Size: circa 180 cm square.

90–92. Irish Regiments in French service
When James II fled to France after the Battle of the Boyne (1690) those Irish regiments which had remained loyal followed him and were re-formed as five regiments in the French service under Colonels Bulkeley, Clare, Dillon, Fitzjames and Roth. All these regiments were named after their colonels.

The colours carried by Clare's and Dillon's regiments were similar to those of Bulkeley's regiment (**91**) except the 1st and 4th quarters were yellow for Clare, black for Dillon, while the 2nd and 3rd quarters were red for both regiments. The colours follow the general pattern for French infantry except they bear a red cross

instead of the white for France, and a device indicating nationality – the lion of England and harp or saltire of Ireland. An Irish cavalry regiment was also raised in 1698 under the command of Fitzjames: this carried a standard of the usual French pattern, described and illustrated under **70**.
Size: (infantry) *circa* 180 cm square.

93–94. French infantry colours
The Régiment de Poitou, originally raised in 1616, carried a very simple colour of the authorized type; the much later Régiment de Chartres, raised in 1691, had to resort to a unique though not complex design of red quarters within a blue border, the white cross of France overall.
Size: in excess of 180 cm square.

95. Holland: Gustaf Mauritz Lewenhaupt's Regt
A company colour of Lewenhaupt's Swedish Regiment, which was in the service of Holland in 1688. The colonel's colour was probably of the design illustrated by **83**. The colour follows a basic pattern for late-seventeenth-century Swedish colours and makes no attempt to indicate the country it served.

96. Holland: infantry colour
The company colour illustrated was carried at the battle of Fleurus in 1690 by one of the infantry regiments of the county of Holland (i.e. the Scheldt and Rotterdam–Amsterdam peninsula) and lost to the French that day. The arms borne in the canton (Or, a

lion rampant Gules) are of the old county of Holland, but whether infantry regiments from the other counties carried similar colours at this date with their arms in the canton is not known for certain, although it is quite likely.

97. Savoy: Marine Regt

Company colour of the Reggimento la Marina, bearing the eagle of Savoy with the country's arms on its breast. Colours of a similar pattern were still being carried by this regiment in the period 1773–93, with the arms of Savoy replaced by two crossed black anchors tied with a gold ribbon, on a white field. The colonel's colour had a quartered shield, 1 and 4 Savoy, 2 and 3 a black anchor on a white field.

98. Holy Roman Empire: infantry colour

Infantry colour carried by troops of the Holy Roman Empire *circa* 1690 and bearing on the shield the arms of the various states.

99–101. Britain: Colours of the Foot Guards

New colours, of a different pattern to any carried before, were presented to the Foot Guards for the coronation of James II in 1685. The colour of the King's Own Company, 1st Foot Guards, was crimson, embroidered in the centre with the royal cypher JR and the imperial crown in gold. The colonel's colour plain crimson, the Lt-Col.'s and all others white with a

St George's cross overall. The Lt-Col.'s also bore in the centre a gold crown; the major's the same but with a pile wavy issuing from the dexter chief of the 1st quarter. 1st Captain's as shown by **100**. 2nd Captain's bore two royal cyphers and crowns; 3rd Captain's three of each, and so on to the 20th Captain, whose cross was charged with twenty cyphers and crowns.

In the Coldstream Regiment the colonel's colour was white, the other eleven colours white with a St George's cross overall. In addition the major's bore a pile wavy; the 1st Captain's as shown by **99**. The 2nd Captain's was as the 1st's but with the numeral II, and so on to the 9th Captain's which bore IX.

The colonel's colour of the Scots Guards was plain white; the Lt-Col.'s a St Andrew's white saltire on a blue field. The major's colour was the same with a pile wavy on the saltire next to the finial. The 1st Captain's colour is shown by **101**. Successive captains probably carried colours with the same numbering system as the Coldstream Regiment.

Sizes: no official sizes were laid down by this date but probably the colours were: Length 247·5 cm. Breadth 225 cm.

102. Britain: The Horse Guards

As explained under **65–66**, each troop had a standard and a guidon. From 1685 the 1st (King's) Troop's were identical to those of the 2nd (Queen's) Troop's, shown here, except there were no angels supporting the crown. 3rd Troop's were of the same design but yellow with silver ornaments; 4th Troop's the same but blue with gold ornaments, except the scroll bearing the motto, which was silver.

Size: (standard only) Length 75 cm. Breadth 71 cm.

103. Britain: Royal Regt of Horse

As senior cavalry regiment the Royal Regiment of Horse had the privilege of a King's Standard, carried by the 1st (King's) Troop. This was crimson, fringed with red and gold, and bore in the centre the king's cypher with a gold crown over, and above the crown a silver scroll bearing the motto DIEU ET MON DROIT. Below the cypher were small crowns as in 102. The colonel's

standard is illustrated here. The Lt-Col.'s bore a rose; the other officers in succession bore a gold thistle, gold fleur-de-lis, gold harp with silver strings, gold oak tree, gold portcullis, and the badge of the Order of the Garter.

Size: Length 75 cm. Breadth 71 cm.

104. Britain: Earl of Shrewbury's Regt of Horse

The colonel's standard of this regiment, later the 5th Dragoon Guards, is illustrated as carried from 1687. The two other troops of the regiment had buff (probably more yellow than buff) standards without any device.

Size: Length 75 cm. Breadth 71 cm.

GREAT NORTHERN WAR 1700–1721

105. Russia: Boris Sheremechev's Cavalry Regt

This standard belonged to a company of the levy of the landed gentry under General Sheremechev. It was captured at Narva in 1700 by the Swedes.

Size: Length 135 cm. Breadth 132 cm.

106. Russia: Alexis Obuchov's Infantry Regt

Czar Peter the Great became suspicious of the power of the Streltzi and in 1698 began to disband the corps by means of deportation and massacres. However, by 1702 the need for soldiers forced him to use the remnants of the corps, restored as four regiments,

one of which was Obuchov's. The colour illustrated was made for a company of this regiment in 1691.

Size: Length 261 cm. Breadth 251 cm.

107–108. Russia: Preobrajenski Life Guards

At the end of the seventeenth century Peter the Great introduced into the Russian Army for the first time a standardized system for flags, following the systems already common in Western Europe. Thus in 1700 the Preobrajenski Life Guards received one white or colonel's colour (107) and fifteen coloured or company colours (108). In other regiments the colonel's colour was also always white, the company colours (one per company) in the colour adopted by the corps. In the Preobrajenski Regiment the 2nd Company colour was identified by one star, 3rd Company by two stars, etc. **108** therefore shows the company colour of the 4th Company.

109. Saxon dragoon guidon
Made about 1700 of silk damask, this guidon was captured by the Swedes during the course of the war. The insignia is virtually unchanged since the

Thirty Years War: the motto means Loyalty is rare.
Size: Length 165 cm (75 cm to the fork). Breadth 100 cm.

110. Swedish artillery standard
This standard dates from 1716. Artillery standards do not appear to have been carried by the men, but rather fixed to a carriage. In the infantry colours continued to be allotted at the rate of one per company until 1731, when a regulation was introduced reducing them to two per battalion.

WAR OF THE SPANISH SUCCESSION 1701–1713

111. Britain: 12th Regt of Foot
Between the restoration of the monarchy in 1660 and the first official regulations for flags in 1743, British colours followed the basic principle of a St George's cross on a coloured field, with devices to distinguish the regiments – most often armorial devices from the colonel's arms. The colonel's colour of the Duke of Norfolk's Regt (12th Foot), *circa* 1686, is typical of colonel's colours of this period. Company colours for this regiment were also red with the St George's cross overall, edged with white. The major's colour also had a pile wavy in white; the 1st Captain a silver cross crosslet fitchée in the centre of the cross. The other captains' colours may have had more crosses or numerals.
Size: probably Length 247·5 cm. Breadth 225 cm.

112. Britain: 1st Royal Regt of Foot
The Lt-Col.'s colour of the regiment from about 1686: the colonel's colour was all white with the same badge in the centre. The major's was as illustrated but with a pile wavy next to the finial; the 1st Captain's had a silver 1 above the badge, and other captains probably used successive numerals.
Size: probably Length 247·5 cm. Breadth 225 cm.

113. Britain: Princess Ann of Denmark's Regt
The major's colour from *circa* 1687. The colonel's colour for this regiment, later the 8th Foot, bore the same insignia on a plain field of the same unique colour. The Lt-Col.'s was as illustrated but minus the pile wavy; the 1st Captain's had a white 1 in the

place of the pile wavy, and the colours of the other captains were numbered in succession.

Size: probably Length 247·5 cm. Breadth 225 cm.

114. Britain: 10th Regt of Foot

Colonel's colour, dating from 1715, of Grove's Regiment, later the 10th Foot. The Union with Scotland in 1707 had a marked effect on the colours of the British Army, the small Union flag being introduced (as shown) to the colonel's colour from that date. The number of colours per regiment was also reduced to three, the 2nd or Lt-Col.'s being the Union flag throughout. The Union also affected the colours of the pre-eminently Scottish colours of the Scots Guards (101), the Royal Regiment (112) and North British Fusiliers, all of which regiments now carried new colours of the English pattern.

Size: probably Length 247·5 cm. Breadth 225 cm.

115. Britain: 3rd Regt of Foot

The 2nd or Union colour of the 3rd Foot in 1709. The WM cypher is from an earlier reign and shows the colour has been altered to incorporate the St Andrew's cross at the Union in 1707. This particular colour was taken by the French at Malplaquet in 1709.

Size: probably Length 247·5 cm. Breadth 225 cm.

116. Britain: Royal Regt of Dragoons

The 1st Captain's guidon, carried from 1687. The regiment had eight troops, each of which carried a guidon. The colonel's was crimson with in the centre the late king's cypher of two letters C interlaced and surmounted by a crown. The embroidery was gold. The Lt-Col.'s guidon bore a gold escarbuncle; 2nd Captain's a rose and pomegranate impaled with green stalk and leaves; 3rd Captain's the rays of the sun rising from a cloud; 4th Captain's the top of a beacon with flames; 5th Captain's a tiger *passant guardant,* spotted with black, yellow and red roundels and breathing red flames, all on a green mound; 6th Captain's a phoenix in flames. All these badges were in the centre of the guidon and surmounted by a gold crown.

Size: probably Length 102·5 cm. Breadth 67·5 cm.

117–122. French colours, standards and guidons

With the exception of the colour of the Régt du Roi, all these flags were captured from the French at the Battle of Blenheim, 1704. The Régt. de Carmen (120) bore a typical cavalry standard of the time, virtually unchanged over the past half century. Other cavalry standards followed approximately the same pattern, some bearing scrolls with mottoes above the sun, some having more ornate borders though still based on four fleur-de-lis. The guidon of the Dragons de la Reine (119) appears to have been the basic pattern of that date, some having the arms of the colonel or province of origin in the centre. The infantry colours, Régt de Laffey (121) and Régt de Tiange (122), are typical of the period and follow the normal French pattern shown at previous dates. The colour of the Régt du Roi (**118**) replaced an earlier colour. (See **63**.) The pattern shown here was carried by the regiment from 1670–1789.

123–124. Spanish infantry colours
Under a decree of 1707 the Spanish Army employed the system of colours now becoming standard throughout most of Europe whereby each regiment had a Sovereign's or colonel's colour and a number of regimental colours. In Spanish regiments each battalion had three colours, and the 1st Battalion carried the colonel's colour. This colour was the same for all regiments and is illustrated by **123**. The regimental colours had fields of the regiment's facing colour or the principal colour of the arms of the city or province where the regiment was raised. In the centre was the name of the unit and a badge, usually the arms of the city or province. The regimental colour illustrated (**124**) belongs to the Irish Waterford Regiment. All four Irish regiments in the Spanish service by 1709 bore a harp as their badge. They carried the normal Royal colour.

125–126. Bavarian colour and standard
The two flags shown were captured at the Battle of Blenheim. The cavalry standard (**126**) employs the colours of the Bavarian arms in a geometric design: the infantry colour (**125**), carried by Colonel d'Amigni's regiment, is of a similar type, utilizing a pattern employed by the Bavarian infantry for the next hundred years.

127. Würzburg cavalry standard
This standard belonged to the Würzburg contingent and dates from 1699–1719. It bears the Imperial eagle with on its breast the arms of Franconia and the city of Würzburg.

128. Prussian infantry colour
A Prussian infantry colour of *circa* 1701. At this date Prussian regiments had a *Leibfahne* or Sovereign's colour, and one *Regimenterfahne* or regimental colour per company. This pattern remained almost unchanged throughout Prussian history, the main changes being to the form of the eagle and the addition of various crosses over the field.
Size: Length 140 cm. Breadth 120 cm.

WAR OF THE POLISH SUCCESSION 1733–1738

129–130. Russian colours, standards and guidons
Under Catherine I each infantry regiment in 1727 received a colonel's colour and six company colours and each dragoon regiment one colonel's and eight squadron guidons. The pattern for the colonel's colour and guidon is

shown in **129**. Fig. 4 illustrates the company or squadron pattern. Each regiment had the fields of the company or squadron flags in its facing colour. Some of these colours were:

Size: Length 190 cm. Breadth 162·5 cm for infantry. Length 145 cm. Breadth 100 cm for dragoons. Cavalry standards were square and much smaller.

INFANTRY

Field	Border	Regiments
Red	Yellow	Belgorodski, Vyborgski
Green	Yellow	Narvski, Nevski
Green	Light blue	Troitski, Vologodski
Yellow	Red	Lefort, Boutyrski, Sibirski, Smolenski, Voronejski, Riazanski, Rostovski, Permski

DRAGOONS

Field	Border	Regiments
Yellow	Green	Iambourg
Green	Red	Narvski, Olonetski, Novotroitski
Red	White	Iaroslavski
Yellow	Red & Green	Kazanski, Viatski, Smolenski

In 1731 the cuirassier regiments were issued with one colonel's standard and a squadron standard per

Fig. 4

squadron. The squadron standard is shown by **130**: the colonel's was of the same pattern but with the usual white field.

131. France: Cuirassiers du Roi
This standard was carried by the Cuirassiers du Roi *circa* 1735 and follows approximately the basic design introduced a century before; see **70**.

132. Austrian hussar standard
A 'standard' carried by Austrian hussars *circa* 1720. The flag is in fact of guidon form, this type of fly being known as wavy-leech.

133. Saxon cavalry standard
The Sovereign's standard for Saxon cavalry regiments, issued in 1735 and carried until 1810.

134. Spanish cavalry standard
Under a decree issued in 1728 each squadron of hussars, dragoons and line cavalry was to have one red standard, the obverse as illustrated, the reverse bearing a trophy of arms and the regiment's number. This pattern was carried right through the eighteenth century and Napoleonic Wars of the early nineteenth century. For the artillery pattern carried over a similar period see **279**.

WAR OF THE AUSTRIAN SUCCESSION 1740–1748

135–137. Spanish colours
The colonel's colour of the Regiment de Badajoz (**135**) should have followed the 1707 pattern illustrated by **123** but in fact the two illustrations have little in common. In 1728 a new regulation decreed the colonel's colour should be as illustrated in **136**. (The reversal of the arms of Spain is because **135** and **136** show the reverse and obverse of the two flags respectively.) Each battalion within a regiment had two colours, the 1st Battalion having the colonel's colour and one battalion colour. Battalion colours were also white and bore the red cross raguly of Burgundy (**137**). Note the irregularity of the branches on the cross. Regiments were allowed to add to either type of colour the arms of the province they represented, but the arms had to be placed at the corners. These regulations remained in force until 1768.

138. France: Hussards de Chamborant
The guidon carried by this regiment in 1744. As with the Austrian hussar flag shown in **132**, the French hussars appear at this date to have carried guidons as opposed to standards, and this basic pattern was carried by many French hussar regiments at this date.

139. France: Gardes Françaises
This colour follows the usual pattern for French infantry with a blue field for a royal regiment. The fleur-de-lis and crowns are typical privileges granted to elite regiments. Founded in 1558 as the Garde du Roi, the regiment was much pampered by the French kings but, although it fought bravely in many great battles, such as Fontenoy in 1745, it was among the first to embrace the cause of the Revolution.

Size: approximately 180 cm square.

140. Lübecker Burgerwehr
A colour carried by the Burgerwehr of Lübeck, the leading town of the Hanseatic League. The colour bears the Imperial eagle with the arms of Lübeck on its breast.

141–144. Prussian colours and guidons
As stated under **128**, Prussian infantry regiments of the eighteenth century

had one *Leibfahne* per regiment and one *Regimenterfahne* per company: thus the 1st Battalion carried a colonel's colour and four regimental colours, the 2nd Battalion five regimental colours. The company colour for the 10th (von Holstein) I.R. illustrated by **143** is of the 1729 issue, the only real difference to the colour illustrated earlier being the use of a wavy cross over the field. (See also **170–72**.) The colour of the 1st Brandenburg Pioneer Battalion (**144**) was issued on 25 November 1741 and follows the same principles.

141 illustrates a typical dragoon guidon of the 1740–86 period; **142** a hussar guidon of 1741–3. The Leib-squadron of this regiment carried a colonel's guidon of the same pattern but reversed colouring, i.e. white with blue border, blue centre with white scroll. Such colour reversal was normal for *Leib-* and *Regimenterfahnen.* Staves were of brown wood, the finial gilt, and cords of black and silver.

Size: (infantry colours) Length 140 cm. Breadth 120 cm.

145–146. Modena: Regg'to Reggio

At the outbreak of the War of the Austrian Succession Modena remained neutral but when her neutrality was violated she joined Spain. By 1740 the duchy was out of the war but a small force continued to fight for Spain and in 1745 the duke was appointed generalissimo of Spanish troops in Italy. The Regiment Reggio was raised on 1 June 1740, the first of five militia regiments taking the names of towns or regions of the duchy. Each of the regiments had three colours, the colonel's (**145**), carried by the first company and of the same pattern for all regiments, and two *Ordinanza* or regimental colours of the pattern shown by **146**.

147–148. British dragoon guidons

This regiment was the Queen's Own Royal Regt of Horse prior to 1746 but from that year became the 2nd Dragoon Guards and therefore carried guidons. The 1st guidon is illustrated by **147**. The 2nd guidon was blue with crown and GR as illustrated in **147** but with a central badge of the Union rose and thistle on one stalk. The 3rd guidon is shown by **148**. The guidons illustrate the design used on both guidons and standards at that date. New regulations were introduced in 1747 but regiments were reluctant to change or uncertain of the changes required, and not until the regulations were reissued in 1751 was there any noticeable change in the design for guidons and standards.

Size: Length 102·5 cm. Breadth 67·5 cm.

149–150. British infantry colours

The first official regulations governing the design of British colours appeared in 1743 but the details were not clearly defined and little change occurred until improved regulations were issued in 1747. For the first time they listed the regimental badges which might be used and illustrated their position and design. The other main feature of the regulations was the reduction of colours to two per regiment, the 1st or King's colour (the Union flag) and the 2nd or Regimental colour (in the facing colour of the regiment except where that colour was red or white, when white was used with the St George's cross overall, and a Union flag in the canton).

149 illustrates the King's colour for the 9th Foot: the Regimental colour had the Union in the canton and the same central device on a yellow (facing colour) field. These colours are typical of the simple design now officially laid down.

150 shows the regimental colour for the 2nd Foot in 1747. The regiment's lamb badge has no traceable history but may have been associated with Queen Catherine: the letters CARA stand for Carolina Regina.

Size: Length 195 cm. Breadth 185 cm.

151–152. Austrian infantry colours

In 1741 Marie Theresa issued regulations for army colours, stating the 1st Battalion of a regiment would carry a *Leibfahne* and a *Regimenterfahne*, other battalions two *Regimenterfahnen* each. **151** shows the obverse and **152** the reverse of the *Leibfahne*. (The sleeve should appear on the right of the flag in **152**, the border on the left.) Hungarian regiments carried a slightly different *Leibfahne*, the design being as shown in **151** but with a green white/red border. (See **175**.) These designs were first listed in an ordinance of 1754 but were in use before that date.

Size: Length 180 cm. Breadth 140 cm.

JACOBITE REBELLION 1745–1746

153. England: King's Own Royal Regt

The colonel's colour of this regiment (Barrel's Blues) as carried at the Battle of Culloden. The 2nd colour was the Union throughout, with in the centre the same crossed sceptres surmounted by the royal crest of England (a crowned lion *statant guardant*, standing upon a royal crown). These colours date from an earlier period and do not conform to the royal warrant of 1743.

Size: Length 195 cm. Breadth 165 cm.

154. England: 3rd Regt of Foot

Regimental colour of the 3rd Foot (The Buffs) showing the ancient

dragon badge of the regiment, officially recognized by the warrant of 1747. The colour may have carried a white scroll above the dragon with the motto *Veteri Frondescet Honore*, but this was not authorized at that date. The regimental colour remained almost unchanged for over half a century and in 1807 bore the motto described below the dragon, and in place of the numeral III the inscription 3rd Regt or Buffs (in three lines) in a red oval surrounded by a gold edge in the centre of the small Union. The colour remained otherwise unchanged. The disputed scroll then disappeared from the colour until 1890, when it was at last officially recognized.

Size: Length 195 cm. Breadth 185 cm.

155. Scotland: Prince Charles Stuart's standard

This standard, or one very like it, was raised at Glenfinnan in Inverness-shire on 19 August 1745 and was the personal standard of Prince Charles, following the medieval or feudal practice. (The standard illustrated was reconstructed by The Lyon King of Arms in 1945.)

Size: Length 8 metres. Breadth 270 cm.

156. Scotland: Lord Ogilvy's Regt

The colour of the 2nd Battalion, carried at Culloden. The colonel's colour was white and of much the same design as **157** except a gold chain surrounds the centre emblem and bears an oval medallion on which is St Andrew with a cross. Another Scottish colour to survive the burning of captured colours (at Edinburgh after the battle) was the regimental colour of Stewart of Appin's Regiment. This was of light blue silk with a yellow St Andrew's saltire overall.

Size: Length 200 cm. Breadth 150 cm.

157. Scotland: Royal Écossais

Three regiments were raised in France to support the rising of the Scottish highlanders, the Royal Écossais in 1744, and Ogilvy and Albany Regiments in 1745, but only small detachments served in the rising. The colour shown is the colonel's. The Albany Regiment's was probably similar.

Size: circa 180 cm square.

FRENCH INDIAN WARS 1754–1763

158–159. Britain: 1st Royal Scots

Under the 1747 warrant the two colours of this regiment were described as shown, the 2nd Battalion's King's colour identified from that of the 1st Battalion by a pile wavy (**158**) and the Regimental colour of the 1st Battalion identified by the numeral in the Union. The plain central badge was usual for royal regiments at this time. The crowned thistle on the Regimental colour had been the badge of the regiment since at least 1684.

Size: Length 195 cm. Breadth 185 cm.

160. Britain: 27th Inniskilling Regt

Regimental colour of the regiment as it appeared in 1747. The regimental number was so placed on colours where the centre of the field was occupied by a royal or regimental badge. According to tradition the badge was conferred by William III.

Size: Length 195 cm. Breadth 185 cm.

161. Britain: 44th Regt of Foot

Regimental colour with the simple central wreath of the 1747 warrant.

This type of wreath was used until *circa* 1760. The King's colour would have been the Union throughout with the central device from the regimental colour in the centre of the St George's cross.

Size: Length 195 cm. Breadth 185 cm.

162. Britain: 55th Regt of Foot

Regimental colour illustrating a rococo design for the central device, a style which came into fashion *circa* 1760 and lasted about twenty years. Some regiments replaced the wreath with the belt of the Order of the Garter during this period. The King's colour was the Union throughout with the wreath and regimental number in the centre.

Size: Length 195 cm. Breadth 185 cm.

163. Britain: 62nd Royal American Regt

King's colour of the 4th Battalion, as issued on its formation in 1756. The regiment was not in the 1751 warrant but should have followed the patterns laid down. However, the colours survive and show they were different to any established pattern. The Regimental colour was of blue silk, with the Union in the canton and the regiment's number in the centre of that Union. The same central badge is on the King's colour except 4 is shown as IV instead of IIII.

Size: Length 195 cm. Breadth 187·5 cm.

Other colonial troops had no recognized colours, except Maryland,

where the arms of Lord Baltimore were carried (Fig. 5), and Rhode Island, whose troops campaigning in Canada in 1746 carried a blue signal flag bearing a white disc.

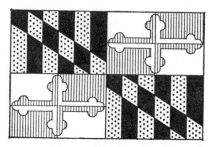

Fig. 5

164–169. French infantry colours

In 1755 six battalions of infantry were despatched to protect the French colonies in America, the regiments de la Reine, Artois, Guyenne, Languedoc, Béarn and Bourgogne. Two battalions of La Sarre and Royal Roussillon were sent a year later, with Montcalm, and several others were also involved in the campaigns. Artois, Bougogne (see **87**) and Cambis garrisoned the great fortress of Louisbourg in what is now Nova Scotia.

All the colours illustrated followed the basic patterns for infantry introduced in the previous century. Régt de Béarn (**167**) was the only regiment to bear the variant illustrated, as was de la Reine (**169**). The pattern used by the Régt de Royal Roussillon (**168**) was shared by Royal (1 and 4 dark violet, 2 and 3 coffee brown); Royal La Marine (1 and 4 sky blue, 2 and 3 orange); and Royal Barrais (1 and 4 black, 2 and 3 yellow). Artois and Languedoc had plain cantons: the former 1 and 4 yellow, 2 and 3 bright blue; the latter 1 and 4 russet, 2 and 3 violet. An order of 10 February 1749 officially reduced the number of colours per battalion to two: the 1st Battalion carried the colonel's colour and one *drapeau d'ordonnance*, other battalions carried two *drapeaux d'ordonnance*.

Size: approximately 180 cm square.

SEVEN YEARS WAR 1756–1763

170–172. Prussian infantry colour
170 shows the *Leibfahne* of Infantry Regt No. 1, the basic pattern used by a large number of regiments. The *Regimenterfahne* for this regiment was orange with orange scroll on a white centre field, otherwise as for *Leibfahne*. From this it may be seen the only variation was an interchange of colour between *Leibfahne* and *Regimenterfahne*: white field for the former and company colour for the centre; company colour for the field of the latter with a white centre. Colours for some other regiments using this pattern were: No. 2, black; No. 3, yellow; No. 41, yellow. Other regiments with the same pattern but with silver used in place of gold, were: Nos. 10 and 43, light green; No. 14, purple; No. 38, red.

A variant employing a form of cross known as a *Keilen* is shown by **171**, the regimental colour of Infantry Regt No. 7. The same principle is applied as for **170**, with an extra colour introduced for the cross, the cross remaining the same colour on both colours. Thus the *Leibfahne* for this regiment would be white with a blue middle field and purple *Keilen*. A *Flammenkreuz* is introduced in the variant illustrated by **172**, the *Leibfahne* of Infantry Regt No. 4. The same principle applies, the *Flammenkreuz* did not change colour, and therefore the *Regimenterfahne* of this regiment was purple with a purple motto scroll, white middle field and yellow *Flammenkreuz*. Dragoons carried the same patterns but in guidon form.

Size: Length 140 cm. Breadth 120 cm.

173. Saxon artillery standard
Sovereign's standard for artillery as issued in 1753. Standards of this pattern were carried by the artillery until 1810, when they were handed in and not replaced.

174–175. Austrian infantry colours
The *Regimenterfahne* for Austrian infantry had an obverse as shown by **174** and reverse as in **152**. Hungarian infantry had a slightly different *Regimenterfahne*, both sides being as shown by **175**. (The field of the 4th quarter on the shield should be red.) The stave for all infantry colours usually had a yellow/black spiral pattern with

121

a gilt finial. Cords were gold or silver, depending on button colour.

Size: Length 180 cm. Breadth 140 cm.

176–181. French infantry colours

Illustrated here are more variations of the basic pattern. The Régiments de Cosse Brissac (**176**) and Limousin (**179**) were the only regiments to carry these variations. The Régiment de Cambresis carried colours of the same pattern as Saintonge (**177**) but with 1 and 4 red/green/red/yellow, 2 and 3 yellow/red/green/red. Régiment de Foix carried colours of the same pattern as Briqueville (**178**) but with yellowy grey and green instead of black and red.

The Grenadiers de France had a complex colour, as might be expected of an elite regiment, following the usual pattern but the field semée of fleur-de-lis and flaming grenades and the arms of France in the centre. The Royal Polish Regiment (**181**) did not follow the French pattern but carried the arms of France and the Polish eagle at the corners and in the centre the sun in its splendour, associated with French military flags since the reign of le Roi-soleil.

Size: circa 180 cm square.

182–183. British Foot Guards

On union with Scotland in 1707 the colours of the Foot Guards were altered to carry the new Union, as in the Line regiments. In 1728 the 1st Foot Guards carried the Royal Standard, a crimson colonel's colour, and twenty-six others bearing the Union. The colonel's colour of the Coldstream Guards was also crimson, the other fifteen colours of the regiment following the general pattern of James II's time. (See **99–101**.) The star of the Order of the Garter was granted as the badge of the Coldstream Guards sometime in the first half of the century, although its first appearance on the colonel's colour is not until 1750.

Even after the 1743 warrant the Guards colours remained basically unchanged. From this date the 1st Foot Guards had a King's Standard, carried only on state occasions, a King's colour for each of the three battalions (**182**, the King's Colour of the 2nd Battalion, issued in 1751 or 1758), and a 'regimental' colour for each battalion, this being one of the old company colours, which were carried in turn as the battalion colour. The 1st Captain's colour was the Union with the company badge (crest of England surmounted by a crown) in the centre and the numeral I in the canton. The other twenty-three companies followed the same pattern with their respective badges and consecutive numbers. A little later the 2nd and 3rd Battalions' King's colours were changed to plain crimson, the 3rd Battalion's distinguished by a pile wavy issuing from the corner of the canton.

The 2nd (Coldstream) Guards carried the following: King's colour for each of the three battalions, crimson with (1st) star of the Garter with crown over it; 2nd, as 1st but with Union in the canton and belt of Order of Garter round a smaller star; 3rd, as 2nd but with pile wavy. The fifteen company colours were the Union with the company badge and crown in the centre and company number in the canton. **183** shows the company colour of the 11th Company, 2nd Guards, *circa* 1758. This regiment did not have a Royal Standard.

Size: 247·5 cm. Breadth 225 cm. After 1747, Length 195 cm. Breadth 185 cm.

184–187. Russian colours, standards and guidons

Under Elisabeth Petrovna each battalion of infantry had two colours, each company of dragoons and Grenadiers à Cheval had one standard or guidon, each squadron of cuirassiers had one standard, and each company of hussars and Pandours had one standard. Artillery had one standard per regiment. The white or colonel's colour was white, the others in the colour adopted by the corps commander, but the devices on all were the same: the Imperial eagle on the colonel's colour, the arms of the city or province after which the regiment was named on the battalion colour. If a regiment had no right to such arms, the Imperial cypher was carried instead.

The basic pattern for the Regt des Gardes à Cheval is given in **184** (colonel's colour of 1742). There were four red company colours with a gold crown and cypher on an orange background, surrounded by a green wreath tied with a light blue ribbon. The gold cypher was repeated on its orange field at each corner. The pattern for the 1st Regt of Grenadiers is given in **185** (company colour of 1756). The regiment had one colonel's and three company colours, the former all white. The line infantry regiments in this period (1741–61) carried the basic pattern illustrated in **186**. The colour of the field and flames at each corner were decided by the commander of the regiment, but the Imperial cypher was always as shown. The Semenovski Life Guards had one colonel's and five company colours, the former being as the company colours (**187**) of 1742, except in white. The colours of the three regiments of Life Guards were distinguishable only by their borders; light blue for Semenovski, red for Preobrajenski, bright green for Ismailovski.

Size: probably the same for all infantry, though the Grenadiers may have had longer colours. Length 213 cm. Breadth 142 cm.

BRITISH WARS IN INDIA   1757–1826

188–190. British and Indian Army infantry colours

In 1757 the Bengal Native Infantry had ten companies (two grenadier) per battalion and each company carried a colour in the regiment's facing colour, with in the centre a device such as a sabre, dagger, crescent, etc. Grenadier companies also had the Union flag in the canton. In 1759 the Madras Army colours were a red cross of St George on the following fields: 1st Battalion, blue; 2nd, yellow; 3rd, green; 4th, black, 5th Battalion had a red field and white cross; 6th, three parallel diagonal stripes red/yellow/red; 7th, the same but red/green/red.

The new Bengal Army corps of 1763 carried the flag of St George. The company system was abolished not long after (1773 for Bengal Army, *circa* 1777 for Madras Army) and by 1781 all Indian Army regiments carried two colours per battalion and followed the British pattern.

Size: Length 210 cm. Breadth 195 cm.

Some examples of the colours carried by British regiments serving in India during this period are illustrated.

191. Britain: 19th Light Dragoons

This regiment embarked for England from India in 1806 after an absence of twenty-four years. On 16 April 1807, together with the 74th and 78th Highlanders, it was authorized to bear an elephant badge with Assaye on its guidons in memory of its glorious part in that battle, and soon afterwards a set of four guidons was made displaying the new badge and motto. These guidons were carried until disbandment in 1821. The illustration shows the guidon of the 4th Squadron. The royal guidon of the regiment was red with the Union badge (rose, thistle and shamrock on one stalk) in the centre, the motto HONI SOIT QUI MAL Y PENSE on a blue ribbon, crown over. In the 1st and 4th corners was the white horse of Hanover, in the 2nd and 3rd XIXLD on a red ground within a small Union wreath. This pattern was carried by all mounted regiments and replaced the pattern illustrated in **147-8**, which was carried until *circa* 1751. The pointed ends of the guidon were authorized in 1768 but many appeared with rounded ends in the Napoleonic Wars and until no longer carried in battle.

Size: (standards) Length 72·5 cm. Breadth 67·5 cm. (guidons) Length 102·5 cm. Breadth 67·5 cm. (Light dragoons probably Length 85 cm. Breadth 70 cm.)

192. French Corps

This colour is typical of French colours during the early part of the Revolutionary Wars and is believed to have belonged to the French European Corps in the service of Tippoo Sahib in the campaign of 1792.

193. French infantry colour

This colour was carried in the 1st Mahratta War (1779–82) and is typical of pre-Revolution French colours. Colours of this pattern, but without the Indian snake, were also carried by the Gatinois and Auxerrois regiments. (See **226**.) In the earlier wars of 1760–1 Lally Tollendal's Irish Regiment, units of the Artillerie du Roi (see **117**) and Régt de Lorraine **(64)** also fought in India against Britain. Lally's regiment was raised in 1744, disbanded in 1763, and carried colours of the pattern shown for Bulkeley's Irish Regt **(91)** with the green and red quarters reversed and without a crown over the harp.

194–195. Standards of Mysore

These standards were carried before the Sultan Hyder Ali and his son and heir Tippoo Sahib and were captured at the storming of Seringapatam in 1799. The palace standard, of light green silk with a red hand in the centre, was also taken.

196. Howdah banner of Mysore

There were two banners of this design, fastened to front and rear of the howdah of Hyder Ali's elephant. These banners were also taken at Seringapatam in 1799.

197. Gurkha colour

This colour was captured at Muckwampore in February 1816, during the Nepal War, from a famous battalion of Gurkhas which was literally destroyed in the battle.

198–199. Bengali standards

Standards of the usurper Doorjun (or Durgan) Sal, 1825–6, taken at the storming of Bhurtpore in the upper provinces of Bengal in January 1826.

200–201. East Indian standards

The colours of these standards, housed at Chelsea Hospital, London, are now uncertain because of fading but they appear to have been red. Other standards of this type to survive are red and bear a black and gold snake. Many Indian flags bear the device of a hand as it was traditional for a Rajah to dip his hand in paint and stamp its imprint on all standards before they were delivered to his regiments.

POLISH STRUGGLE FOR INDEPENDENCE 1768–1794

202–203. Polish standard and colour

Illustrated are a standard carried by Polish irregulars (Kosyniers) led by Kosciuszko during the national rising against partition by Prussia and Russia (202) and the colour carried by the Krakow Grenadiers about the same period, 1792–4 (203).

204–205. Prussian colours

Two variants of the basic infantry pattern illustrated by 170–172. A *Johanniterkreuz* has been added to the colour of Infantry Regt No. 19 (204);

the *Regimenterfahne* had the same colours but reversed. This pattern was also carried by Infantry Regt No. 34 (white field and blue cross for *Leibfahne*, blue with white cross for *Regimenterfahne*), but the cypher, wreath and grenades were silver instead of gold.

Infantry Regt No. 15 (205) was the only regiment to carry this variant. The *Regimenterfahne* was similar but with a blue inner field and silver scroll.

Size: Length 140 cm. Breadth 120 cm.

206. Russia: Novgorodski Cuirassier Regt

This regiment received one colonel's and four squadron standards under Peter III. The colonel's was white with yellow corners; the squadron standards being as shown. The motto reads: JE NE CRAINS PERSONNE. The same pattern was carried by line cavalry and line infantry (one colour per company) with the colour for the company colours or standards decided by the commander of the corps.

Size: (infantry) Length 213 cm. Breadth 142 cm.

207. Russia: Preobrajenski Life Guards

Under Catherine the Great the royal cypher changed from 1762 and the Preobrajenski Life Guards were issued with a colonel's and sixteen company colours. The colonel's colour is shown here: the fields of all company colours were black. Those of the other Life Guards (one colonel's and twelve company colours) followed the same pattern but were distinguished by different coloured corners: Semenovski, bright blue; Ismailovski, bright green.

Size: probably Length 213 cm. Breadth 142 cm.

AMERICAN WAR OF INDEPENDENCE 1775–1783

208–213. British infantry colours

Another royal warrant dealing with colours was issued in 1768. Details were basically the same as the 1743 and 1747 warrants but for the first time were mentioned regiments with black facings (St George throughout on a black field with a small Union flag in the canton) and the exact size. Full details of the devices were listed but as the colours were ordered by the colonel of each regiment variations continued to occur, as shown by the colours illustrated. By the 1780s the more flamboyant central cartouche and wreath had been abandoned and a more symmetrical but larger shield came into fashion, with a formal edging and a simple Union wreath. However, in Scottish regiments a variety of designs remained in use; see also **188**.

The King's (**208**) and regimental (**209**) colours of the 9th Foot, dating from 1772 and typical of that date, illustrate how designs could vary not only from regiment to regiment but also within a regiment. (The centre of the regimental colour was probably cut from an older colour, *circa* 1757.) **210** illustrates the 1771 regimental colour of a regiment with red facings: regiments with white facings followed the same pattern. The use of Arabic numerals, on the 1780 regimental colour of the 103rd Foot (**212**), was most unusual at this date.

Size: Length 195 cm. Breadth 180 cm.

214–215. Brunswick colours

Basically the first colour of the Brunswick regiments in North America was in the regiment's facing colour with a cross in white. The second colour reversed this. However, not all regiments followed this arrangement. Illustrated are the 2nd colour of von Rhetz Regt (**214**), facing colour white and using green as a contrasting colour, and the 1st colour of von Specht Regt (**215**), facing colour red. Von Riedesel had yellow facings but carried a blue cross; Prinz Frederick also had yellow facings but carried a black cross.

216. Hesse-Hanau colours
2nd or regimental colour of the Erbprinz Regt, the only Hesse regiment to serve in North America. The 1st colour bore the full arms and supporters of Count Wilhelm of Hesse-Hanau on a pink field.

217. Anspach-Bayreuth colours
There were two Anspach-Bayreuth regiments in North America (1st and 2nd), each having five companies and every company carrying a colour. The obverse for all was as illustrated: the reverse is shown by Fig. 6. This was also white with all gold ornaments, except the wreath, which was green. MZB stands for Markgraf zu Brandenburg.

218–219. Hesse-Cassel colours
Each regiment had two colours, the first in the facing colour with a white cross, the second reversing this. Other emblems were as shown. Facing colours were red for Garde Grenadier companies and Mirbach; crimson for

Bunan and Jäger; black for Knyphausen and Heldring; yellow for Hyne; aurore for Kreis; orange for Stein. Two exceptions to this general rule, where white crosses are not used, were Prinz Carl (**218**) and the Leib du Corps (**219**). In both cases the 1st colour is shown. The 2nd colour of Prinz Carl was all green.

220. North America: Washington's Guard
Small groups of soldiers from each of the colonies were attached to Washington to form this regiment, which

Fig. 6

fought alongside other troops in battle. The colour illustrated was probably designed in 1782 as it bears the eagle, which was not made official until then.

221. North America: Philadelphia Light Horse
This colour was presented to the 1st Troop in 1775 and for many years it was thought this was the first flag to bear the stripes of the United States. However, a scrutiny of the original reveals that this was an old British

colour for the militia, and the stripes have been painted over the Union flag in the canton. The monogram LH above the horse's head simply represents Light Horse.

Size: Length 105 cm. Breadth 92 cm.

222. North America: 2nd Regt Light Dragoons

This regiment was originally led by Major Sheldon of Connecticut but was later commanded by Major Tallmadge of New York and became famous as Tallmadge's Dragoons. It fought at Brandywine, Germantown and Monmouth. A second standard survives with a blue field and '2- Reg^t Lt Dragoons' over the central emblem.

Size: 76 cm square.

223. North America: Webb's Continental Regt

The colour illustrated is usually attributed to the 1st Company of an additional Continental Regt of Foot raised in 1777 by Colonel Webb of Connecticut – the 3rd Connecticut Regt. However, in May 1776 the colours of the Connecticut regiments were reorganized with fields of different colours, the 1st Regt having a yellow field, and the colour may have belonged to this regiment. The size suggests the colour was in fact some sort of guidon.

Size: 92 cm square. A full size colour (1·83 metres square) for Webb's Regt has survived; this is also yellow, with a blue scroll over an Indian bearing a gold shield. At his feet

is an unidentifiable animal standing over the head of the King of England.

224. North America: 1st Continental Regt of Foot

This regiment was raised in Pennsylvania by order of Congress in 1776 for the Army of the United Colonies and consisted mainly of Pennsylvanian frontier riflemen: it was commonly known as the 1st Pennsylvanian Rifles. The regiment was captured in December 1776 at Fort Washington.

225. North America: Pulaski's Legion

Embroidered for Count Pulaski's independent corps of light cavalry and infantry by the Moravian Sisters of Bethlehem, Pennsylvania in 1778, this standard was carried in many battles before Pulaski's death at Savannah in 1779. The reverse bore the monogram US and around it the motto UNITA VIRTUS FORCIOR [sic]. The standard, which survives in a faded state, was probably red originally.

Size: 46 cm square.

226–231. French infantry colours

Although the 1749 order specified there should be only two colours per battalion, some regiments were still carrying one per company as late as the 1770s. Designs remained basically unchanged and some different variants are illustrated. The *drapeaux d'ordonnance* of the Régiment d'Auxerrois was as for Gatinois (**226**) but with the colours blue and green (blue uppermost in 1 and 4, the reverse in 2 and 3). This pattern was also carried by a French unit in India (**193**) and appears to have been introduced sometime during the second half of the century. The Île de France Regiment, which did not serve in America, carried colours of the same pattern as Hainault (**227**) but with black triangles pointing upwards on yellow fields. The Régt d'Agenois (**228**) appears to have been the only regiment to carry the pattern shown,

again introduced after the Seven Years War.

The famous Lauzun Legion may have had infantry colours with the quarters 1 and 4 blue, 2 and 3 green – the same as the Régt Marine Sayonne, which also served in America. The hussars of the legion may have had a standard based on the Lauzun arms: a grey field, fringed gold, and bearing in the centre a shield quartered red and gold, supported by two griffins and with a gold crown above. *Size:* (infantry) 162 cm square.

FRENCH REVOLUTIONARY AND NAPOLEONIC WARS 1792–1815

232–237. Austrian colours and standards

The *Leibfahne* and *Regimenterfahne* patterns in use in the Seven Years War (**174** and **175**) and War of the Austrian Succession (**151** and **152**) remained in use until 1781 when Joseph II, successor to Marie Theresa, ordered the army's flags to be altered. Besides the new cypher JII there were drastic changes in the arms on the shield on the eagle's breast, as illustrated by the *Regimenterfahne* for infantry regiments for the period 1792–1804 (**233**). This was issued under Franz II (1792–1835) but those issued in 1781 were identical apart from the cypher. The *Leibfahne* still bore the Madonna on a white field (**151**), but the reverse was now as the *Regimenterfahne* but on a white field. The basic pattern for cavalry standards during this period is shown by **236**. The *Leibstandarte* carried by cavalry regiments

from 1780–1898 may be seen under **362**.

The Austrian army was a heterogeneous collection of nationalities, drawn from all parts of the Empire, and among the regiments were Walloon ones raised in the Austrian Netherlands. Their *Regimenterfahne* for the period 1768–97, after which Austria lost the Netherlands to France, is illustrated in **232**.

The next drastic change was brought about by the defeat at the hands of Napoleon and the ending of the Holy Roman Empire. The arms on the eagle's breast were now changed to show the territorial adjustments. The new *Regimenterfahne* for 1804–6 is illustrated by **234**. This was replaced in 1806 by the one shown in **235**, which was used until 1816. The *Leibfahne* was as before for the obverse (the Madonna) with the reverse as **235** but on a white field.

The regimental number was carried in each of the top corners on a small rectangle of cloth sewn to the field, thus 'I.R. N$^{o.}$' (in two lines). The basic pattern for cavalry standards, 1806–16, is shown in **237**.

Size: infantry, Length 180 cm. Breadth 140 cm; cavalry, varying from Length 70–80 cm. Breadth 63–70 cm.

238. Britain: 1st Royals

Regimental colour of the 1st Battalion *circa* 1790, probably replaced soon after the union with Ireland in 1801. It shows the appearance of colours just before the Union. The wreath is unusual for royal regiments at this date, which generally bore the Garter emblem. The cypher is also rather fancy. The King's colour bore the same central device on the Union, but without the thistle badges at the corners.

Size: Length 195 cm. Breadth 180 cm.

239. Britain: Coldstream Guards

Royal standard presented by Queen Charlotte towards the end of the eighteenth century. Originally the standard bore only the central Garter star (regimental badge), wreath (without shamrocks), and possibly the crown, but the union with Ireland in 1801 necessitated the introduction of the shamrock. The honour Egypt and the sphinx were probably added at the same time. The honours Lincelles, Talavera and Barrosa were authorized in 1814: Peninsula and Waterloo in 1815–16.

Size: Length 195 cm. Breadth 180 cm.

240. Britain: de Meuron's Swiss Regt

This regiment was raised for the Netherlands service in 1781 by de Meuron of Neuchâtel, but transferred to the British service in 1795 in Ceylon and fought at Seringapatam in 1799. The colour carried at this date was similar to the one shown. The same pattern was used after 1801, but with St Patrick's saltire added to the canton.

Size: Length 170 cm. Breadth 120 cm.

241. Britain: 23rd Light Dragoons

The Royal guidon of 1815 is illustrated; the regiment's other guidons were blue. The 23rd was raised originally as the 26th but was renumbered in 1803. All the guidons were made soon after the renumbering, and the honours Peninsula, Talavera and Waterloo would have been added in 1815–16. The regiment was converted to lancers towards the end of 1816 and guidons were no longer carried. It is not known for sure if cavalry regiments carried their standards and guidons in the field during the earlier phases of the Peninsula War but they were not carried in 1812 or after.

Size: Length 102·5 cm. Breadth 67·5 cm.

242. Britain: 1st Foot Guards

King's colour of the 3rd Battalion, as carried at Waterloo. The honours

Corunna and Barrosa were conferred on 18 January 1812 and this colour was probably made soon after that date. The regimental colour was the Union with the badge of the 8th Company in the centre, the green dragon of Wales surmounted by a crown.

Size: Length 195 cm. Breadth 180 cm.

243. Britain: King's German Legion

There were eight line and two light battalions in the Legion. The line battalions had two colours each, the 1st being the Union illustrated. (The central inscription reads Kings/German Legion/V Battalion.) The 2nd colour was dark blue (facing colour) with the Union in the canton. The K.G.L. and battalion number were carried in the centre with the Union wreath around them as shown in the illustration. After the Peninsula campaign the honour Peninsula was painted round the wreath. These colours were carried at Waterloo.

Size: Length 195 cm. Breadth 180 cm.

244. France: infantry colours 1791–4

Regimental colour of the 52nd Regt of Infantry (both sides the same); the tricolour in the canton indicates the 1st Battalion. In the early years of the revolution the pattern of the infantry colours remained virtually unchanged from those of the Royal Army, which in the last quarter of the eighteenth century appear to have adopted the fleur-de-lis as an extra badge. The

first change was instituted by a decree of 22 October 1790, which ordered the white cravat to be replaced by a tricolour one. Another decree of 22 November 1792 ordered the fleur-de-lis to be covered by small blue/white/red diamonds.

Size: 180 cm square.

245. France: infantry colours 1794–1804

In early 1794 the old line regiments and national guard battalions were amalgamated to form Demi-Brigades and a decree of 2 March 1794 stated there should be one colour per battalion, this colour to bear on the obverse

Fig. 7. French finial, 1791–94

a lictor's fasces surmounted by a bonnet of liberty and flanked by two branches of oak leaves. 'République Française' appeared on a scroll above the fasces and on the reverse DISCIPLINE ET OBÉISSANCE AUX LOIS MILITAIRES. The number of the Demi-Brigade appeared in each corner on both sides. On the example shown 'Sou-mission' has been used in place of 'Obéissance'. This example is of the 2nd Battalion, 23rd Demi-Brigade, as indicated by the tricolour in the canton, the 1st Battalion now being indicated by a border of blue/white/red. This type of colour was carried until 1804, with a spearhead finial in place of the fleur-de-lis one carried through the eighteenth century, and a tricolour cravat, but there were many geometric variations of this basic pattern, all using blue/white/red in the form of borders or to partition the field itself.

Size: 162 cm square.

246. France: 1804 Eagle
The French eagle of the Napoleonic era had a value far exceeding that of a flag and Napoleon made a point of personally presenting them to his regiments. The first ones were presented to the Army on 5 December 1804 at the Champ de Mars in Paris. There was one eagle for each battalion or squadron. A second distribution to the Army was made on 1 and 4 June 1815 at the Champ de Mai and, during the period of the Empire, Napoleon presented individual eagles at parades in the yard of the Tuileries. A minority of regiments, notably those formed in 1813, received their eagles from the Ministry of War.

The 1804 eagles weighed 1850 grams, had a height of 308–310 mm and a maximum width of 255 mm. The loss of eagles at Wagram and Eylau led to orders forbidding cavalry regiments to carry eagles in Spain, and *all* light horse regiments were

ordered to leave their eagles at their depots. These orders were frequently ignored. For the same reason the number of eagles was reduced to one per regiment in 1806, but this was not put into practice until 1809 in the Army of Germany and not officially decreed until 25 December 1811.

Most eagles were destroyed by the Royalists in 1814 and new ones of a simpler design were cast in 1815. These were more tightly crouched and had a closed beak. 206 were issued on 1 June 1815 and 86 to the National Guard on 4 June. Some regiments had managed to preserve their old eagles and these were carried in 1815 rather than the new ones. This occurred in the 7th, 8th, 29th and 93rd Line, 7th Cuirassiers, 5th Chevau-léger lanciers, and 3rd and 7th Hussars, this last one having belonged originally to the 23rd Chasseurs à Cheval.

247. France: infantry colours 1804
From the end of 1804 to *circa* 1811 the colour illustrated was carried beneath the eagles of the infantry, cavalry and artillery, the only variation being the size and shape for the different arms and the name of the regiment. The reverse, for all except the Guard, was of the same design with 'Valeur et Discipline' in the centre and beneath it the number of the battalion or squadron. Beneath this was added any honour granted to the regiment, but from 1808 these were restricted to major victories of the Empire at which Napoleon had commanded in person, i.e. Ulm, Austerlitz, Jéna, Eylau, Friedland, Eckmühl, Essling, Wag-

ram. The Guard was allowed to carry Marengo.

Officially there were no fringes or cravats but some regiments used the latter and in practice many regiments carried only their eagles on bare staves or kept the colours furled.

Size: infantry 80 cm square; cavalry and artillery 60 cm square.

248. France: infantry colours 1812
By a decree of 25 December 1811 a new *drapeau* was ordered for all branches of the army. The new design was covered with gold embroidery and the bearer had to be changed regularly because of their weight.

Fig. 8

Figure 8 shows the reverse (39th Infantry). The colours were issued in the early summer of 1812 but cavalry were forbidden to take their standards into the field. For the Grande Armée the colours were delivered during the march into Russia, although some regiments appear to have continued to use the earlier pattern.

The obverse and reverse of the 1st Grenadiers' colour are shown by Figs 9 and 10.

Size: infantry 80 cm square; cavalry and artillery 60 cm square.

Fig. 9

249. France: infantry colours 1815
The new *drapeaux* issued in 1815 were of necessity far simpler than the earlier issues but followed the same basic pattern; the red and blue sections were of a paler colour than is shown here; on the reverse were Austerlitz/Jéna/Friedland/Essling/Wagram. The fringe depicted in our illustration is an error. The standard for dragoon regiments in 1815 is illustrated on the cover. (The reverse for this regiment bore the honours Ulm, Austerlitz, Jéna, Eylau.)

Size: infantry, 120 cm square

Fig. 10

(Guard probably 80 cm); cavalry and artillery, 55 cm square.

250–255. Prussian colours, standards and guidons

Generally speaking the flags of the Prussian armies during the 1792–1806 period bore the same patterns as during the eighteenth century: see **170–172, 204–205.** The main changes were in the royal cyphers. Prior to 1792 the number of colours per infantry regiment had been reduced to two per battalion with the *Leibfahne* and a battalion colour carried by the 1st Battalion: other battalions carried two colours known as *Avancierfahne* (1st) and *Retirierfahne* (2nd).

During the campaign of 1806 some 340 colours were lost. A few were saved and handed on to the new army of 1808 but most regiments had to have new flags manufactured. Under a regulation of 27 November 1807 the infantry were to have two colours a battalion, the Grenadier and Fusilier battalions none. Fusiliers were granted colours in 1814 and Grenadiers were carrying them by 1813, usually a *Retirierfahne* of the senior regiment from which their companies were drawn, though in the case of West Prussian and Schlesisches battalions the *Retirierfahne* of the junior regiment was carried. The new colours do not appear to have been ready until the campaign of 1813, when only the *Avancierfahne* of each battalion was carried in the field. Finals were gilt, of spearhead shape, and bore the cypher of the king. Staves were white except for I.R.s Nos. 3, 4, 9, 10 and 11, and the 2nd Grenadier Battalion

and Leib-Grenadier Battalion, which were black. 1st and 2nd Garde Regiments had yellow staves from 13 January 1813 and their finials were silver.

The cavalry and dragoon standards and guidons remained basically unchanged throughout this period, though after 1808 only the dragoons and cuirassier regiments carried them in the field. There was one flag per squadron until 1 October 1811, when a decree called in all flags of regiments on active service except one. Thus in the 1813 campaign regiments carried only one standard or guidon. Uhlan and Hussar regiments were granted the right to carry standards in 1814 but these were not presented until after the peace.

The early hussar flag is illustrated by **251**, presented to the Thuringia Hussar Regt on 30 July 1791. The standard for Guard Cuirassier regiments (and Garde du Corps) from 1798–1899 is illustrated by **253**; that for dragoon regiments by **254** (Litthauisches Dragoner-Regt). The *Ehrenstandarte* (literally standard of honour) is illustrated by **252**, a standard presented to the Dragoner-Regt König (2 Württemberg) No. 26 on 6 December 1805.

Reserve and Landwehr units did not officially carry flags but many carried a large white Teutonic cross on a black field, and Silesian Landwehr apparently carried sky-blue flags with the yellow eagle of Silesia in the centre. **255** illustrates the colour of the Hanseatic Legion in Lübeck in 1813.

Size: infantry, Length 140 cm. Breadth 120 cm.

256. Russia: Semenovski Foot Guards

Until 1796 the Foot Guards carried colours as issued in 1763 (see **207**), but in that year new colours were issued of the pattern illustrated. The colour shown is the company colour; colonel's colours had white instead of yellow crosses. The 'corners' for Preobrajenski were red, green for Ismailovski. In January 1799 the Guards' colours were altered to follow the basic pattern of the Line infantry.

Size: 140 cm square.

ski Grenadiers: rose pink field, black cross, black eagle on orange background, gold crowns, claws, beaks, orb and sceptre, light blue ribbon and green wreath. In 1800 the pattern illustrated by the colour plate was introduced and a system employed whereby the colour allotted to each of the new Inspections replaced the old divisional colours for the field. A company colour for the Orenburg and Siberian regiments is shown. All colonel's colours had a white Maltese cross.

| Inspection | Colonel's Colour 'Corners' | Company Colours | | Embroidery |
		Cross	'Corners'	
Brest, Lithuania, Livonia, Smolensk	black/red	black	red	silver
Dniestr, Caucasus, Crimea, Ukraine	yellow/white	yellow/white	white	gold
Moscow, St Petersburg	L. crimson/white	L. crimson/white	white	gold
Orenburg, Siberia	yellow/green	green	yellow	gold
Finland	black/mid-blue	mid-blue	black	gold

Fig. 11

257. Russia: infantry colours 1800

Under Paul I the pattern illustrated by Fig. 11 was issued in 1797 and carried until 1799. This particular colour was carried by the Malorosii-

The 1797 and 1800 patterns were carried by many regiments throughout the Napoleonic Wars.

Size: 140 cm square.

258. Russia: infantry colour, St George model

On 13 June 1806 the first St George colour was issued (to the Kiev Grenadier Regt), such colours being awarded as a special honour. The example illustrated is for the Fanagoriiski Grenadier Regt and was issued in 1810; that issued to the Kiev Grenadier Regt had a red oval on the eagle's breast, bearing the arms of Moscow – St George slaying the dragon. These arms were not included on later St George colours. The stave finial for these colours had the white cross of the Order of St George painted on, and the cords and cravat

Fig. 12.
Russian
finial, 1797
pattern

were orange and black. From 1807 the divisional system was reintroduced but old Inspection colours continued to be carried and any new ones followed the existing pattern. From 1813 the colonel's colour was no longer issued and company colours were replaced by one per battalion.
Size: 140 cm square.

259. Russia: Dragoons 1797 pattern

The 1797 pattern for dragoon regiments was carried by these regiments until 1803. Each regiment had a colonel's and four squadron standards. The squadron standard illustrated belonged to the Smolensk

Dragoons. Hussars had no standards with the exception of the Pavlovgrad Hussars who were awarded on 13 June 1806 a colonel's and nine squadron standards of St George, i.e. as illustrated but with inscriptions at the edges, see **258**.
Size: 52·5 cm square.

260. Russia: Cuirassier and Dragoon pattern 1803

In 1803 cuirassier and dragoon regiments received a colonel's and four squadron standards of the pattern illustrated. The colonel's was abolished in 1814, otherwise these standards were carried to the end of the Napoleonic Wars. A colonel's standard is illustrated; squadron standards were green for all regiments with a white

Fig 13.
Russian
Chevalier
Gardes,
1800–15.
Three of
these vex-
illum
standards
were carried:
red fields,
white crosses,
gold fringe
and stave, the
latter with
silver fluting,
and silver finial.

background to the corner emblem. The standard carried by cuirassiers from 1797–1803 was of basically the same pattern except the centre emblems were a cross surrounded by rays in the corner nearest the stave, the eagle in the opposite bottom corner facing the cross. There were one colonel's and four squadron standards per regiment.

Size: 1803 pattern, Length 57·5 cm; Breadth 50 cm. 1797–1803 cuirassiers, Length 52·5 cm; Breadth 45 cm.

261. Russia: banner of the Don Cossacks

The banners carried by the Cossacks followed no apparent pattern but all were of the general appearance of the example illustrated, issued in 1803, with various individual emblems in the centre. Some regularity does appear, however, in other aspects of the banners: for example, the finials and fringes were all gold, as was most ornamentation on the banner itself; cords and cravate were silver; while the sleeve was red and the stave green.

262. Baden: infantry colours

The army of Baden fought as allies of Napoleon from 1806 and consisted of four infantry regiments, Garde-du-Corps, cavalry and artillery. The colours carried by the infantry were of the pattern illustrated, differing only in colours. The *Regimenterfahne* were:

Between 1806–8 the regiments also carried a *Leibfahne*, having the colours for field and cross reversed. The 2nd Regt may have carried its *Leibfahne* after 1808.

263. Bavarian infantry colours

The illustration shows the *Bataillonsfahne* issued in 1803 and carried throughout the Napoleonic Wars. The *Leibfahne* was white and bore in its centre the quartered arms of the Electorate of Bavaria, with in the centre a red oval bearing the golden orb of the Elector. These arms were on an ermine mantle and under an electoral cap, flanked by lions and palm and laurel branches. From early 1804 there were one *Ordinärfahne* and one *Leibfahne* per regiment, the latter carried by the 1st Battalion. The electoral cap on the *Leibfahne* was replaced by a crown when Bavaria was made a kingdom in 1806 and in 1808 the arms were simplified to the blue and white *Lozengy in bend* of Bavaria. *Size:* 173 cm square.

264. Brunswick infantry colours

Prior to April 1814, the Brunswick troops did not have colours. The three battalions at Waterloo each carried two flags, a *Herzogsfahne* or

Regiment	Corners or Field	Maltese Cross	Wreath	Cyphers
1st	Red	Yellow	Green	No wreath and corner cyphers reversed
2nd	White	Red	Green	As illustrated
3rd	White	Dark blue	Green	As illustrated
4th	White	Yellow	Gold	As illustrated

Fig. 14

Ordinärfahne of the 2nd Battalion, Prinz Maximilien Regt, carried between 1802–11. Saxon infantry regiments carried two colours, the *Leib-*

Fig. 15

Duke's flag, and a *Bataillonsfahne*. Illustrated is a *Bataillonsfahne*, possibly of the 1st Battalion. The 2nd Battalion's *Bataillonsfahne* appears in Fig. 14 (see jacket illustration for colour details). On the reverse was the cypher FW within a wreath surmounted by a crown, all in silver.

Size: 140 cm square.

The *Herzogsfahne* of the 3rd Battalion had a very wide black border round a light blue centre on which was the white horse of Hanover (in silver) with the motto NUNQUAM RESTORSUM over it in silver. The centre of the reverse was yellow and bore a silver wreath surmounted by a crown and with a silver death's head below. Within the crest in silver letters was MIT GOTT/FÜR FURST/UND/VATERLAND/ MDCCCIV.

Size: 142 cm square.

265. Nassau infantry colour

The colour illustrated dates from 1810 and was carried by Nassau units in the service of France, and at Waterloo by the 1st and 2nd Regiments fighting on the side of the Allies. No other pattern appears to have been issued.

fahne being carried by the 1st Battalion.

Size: Length 157 cm. Breadth 144 cm.

The army was reorganized after the campaigns of 1806–7 and new colours presented on 20 July 1811. The pattern was the same for all regiments, the reverse as Fig. 15, the obverse a crown over a shield bearing the arms of Saxony, couched on a red and ermine mantle. The fields and borders differed for the various regiments: Leib Grenadiers border as Fig. 16i (three light-blue wavy lines, silver foliage, on lemon yellow), field lemon yellow: Prinz Anton border as Fig. 16ii (light blue with gold leaves and bars), field light blue: Prinz Clemens border as Fig. 16ii (light blue with silver leaves and bars), field light blue: Regt Low border as Fig. 16iii (emerald green with silver ornaments), field emerald green.

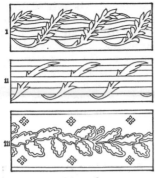

Fig. 16

Size: Length 151 cm. Breadth 146 cm.

The cavalry and artillery standards carried until 1810 are illustrated by **133** and **173** respectively.

267. Würzburg infantry colours

This colour drawing illustrates the pattern for the obverse of colours presented to the two regiments of Würzburg infantry in August 1806 and carried until 1814 when the regiments were incorporated into the Bavarian army and Bavarian colours were issued. The reverse bore either a red F beneath a gold crown within a green laurel wreath, all on a yellow field, or the quartered arms surmounted by a crown and within a red and ermine mantle and green laurel wreath.

Size: Length 160 cm. Breadth 120 cm.

268. Piedmontese infantry colours

One colonel's colour (1st Battalion) and one battalion colour for every other battalion were issued to the Piedmontese regiments *circa* 1780 and these were carried in the Revolutionary Wars. They were basically the same for all regiments, the cavalry and dragoons using the same pattern in standard or guidon form. The obverse of the colonel's colour for the Regg'to de Savoie is shown and Fig. 17 illustrates the reverse. The arms of the regiment were carried in the central cartouche, two alternative examples being given in Fig. 17i (Montferrat) and 17ii (Piémont). Battalion colours were as the reverse of the colonel's colour.

Size: measurements vary slightly in

Fig. 17

surviving colours: Length 168–180 cm. Breadth 183–188 cm.

269. Cispadana Republic: Lombard Legion

The legion had six cohorts, each of which appears to have had its own colours, the 1st Cohort receiving its colour on 7 November 1796. The obverse is shown; the reverse was similar but the inscription reads SUBORDINAZIONE/ALLE LEGGI MILITARI and the two daggers are missing, in their place being LEGIONE LOMBARDA/ COORTE/N° [device] 6.

Size: Length 146 cm. Breadth 132 cm.

270–271. Neapolitan infantry colours

In 1806 the Neapolitan army adopted colours of the French pattern (see **247**), except the blue parts were black. There was one flag per battalion. The obverse of the 1st Light Infantry is shown (**270**); the reverse bore in the centre the inscription: GUISEPPE/NAPOLEONE/RE DELLE DUE SICILIE/AL 1ᵐᵒ REGGIMENTO/D'INFAN-TERIA/LEGGERA.

Size: 80 cm square.

On 15 February 1811, Murat, king of Naples, decreed that new flags be issued. Their border was white and dark purple, diced, the centre of the obverse pale blue with the royal arms, the reverse a garland of oak and laurel leaves in gold around an inscription identifying the regiment. (The outer white border should be in the colour of the field.) The finial was a gilt horse rampant on the capital of a Corinthian column. These colours were carried until 1815. The 7th Real Africano Regt (**271**) was formed from coloured personnel.

Size: Length 85 cm. Breadth 78 cm.

272–273. Kingdom of Italy colours and standards

In 1805 the Republic became a kingdom and flags of the French pattern

were supposed to be carried from that date but most regiments continued to use their republican ones. By 1808 the army had been reorganized and in that year new flags were issued, one per battalion or squadron, the same pattern being used for all arms except those of the cavalry and dragoons were in standard or guidon

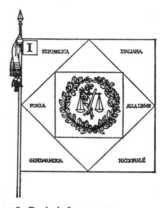

Fig. 18. Basic infantry pattern, Italian Republic, 1802–05. Cavalry standards were similar but with fringes. Corners red, central square olive green, central diamond and small square in canton are white.

form. (See **247**.) However, the Italian flags had green corners instead of blue and on the obverse the inscription read: NAPOLEONE IMPERATORE E RE AL . . . REGGIMENTO FANTERIA DI LINEA (or LEGGERA). In the centre of the reverse was the Imperial eagle, on its breast a red shield bearing a gold crown. Under the shield was another smaller one of light blue bearing a gold N. Above the eagle was VALORE E

DISCIPLINA and beneath it . . . BAT-TAGLIONE on a pale blue label.

For an unknown reason the 1813 standard of the 1st Squadron Dragoni della Regina (**272**) has the colours of the corners reversed. Earlier standards conform to the usual pattern. The slight differences in light cavalry standards are shown by **273**: the reverse bore VALORE E DISCIPLINA with the squadron number below and four golden bugle horns, with the regiment's number on, below the crowns at each corner.

Size: infantry, 80 cm square: dragoons and cavalry, 60 cm square.

274–276. Portuguese colours and standards

During the period 1806–14 the 9th, 11th, 21st and 23rd Regts carried a King's colour as illustrated by **274** with slight differences in the arrangement of the central emblem and its surrounding motto, and the colour of the scroll beneath it. **275** illustrates such a variant, carried by the 21st Regt. Another variant had a sheaf of greenery beneath the central device, bound by long scrolls bearing a motto. The King's colour of the 7th Caçadores is shown by **276**, though a different source gives a colour of the pattern shown in **274**, with the sheaf beneath the central device. Battalion colours were coloured according to division: North, yellow; Centre, white; South, red; and bore in the centre the arms illustrated in **274**, without the surrounding motto, the scroll beneath bearing the regiment's number and the corner cyphers on the field colour.

Cavalry standards, one per squadron, followed the same general pattern as battalion colours except the arms of Portugal were surrounded by a rococo frame and the scroll was blue. The standards were square and smaller than the colours. Their fields were 1st Squadron, white; 2nd, red; 3rd, yellow; 4th, blue.

Aragon *Castile*

Leon *Granada*

Fig. 19.

277–279. Spanish colours and standards

In 1768 a decree stipulated that regiments would carry two flags per battalion, one per squadron. This was reduced to one per battalion on 26 August 1808. The King's colour (1st Battalion) is illustrated by **278**, the colour of the Irlanda Regt. The arms of the regiment's town, province or kingdom (in this case the harp of Ireland) appeared at each corner. (The background to the harps is shown as both green and blue. The latter perhaps being a faded green.) Fig. 19 gives some other examples of typical arms. Battalion colours were as in **277**, again with a coat of arms in the corners: a battalion colour of the Macarquibir Regt is illustrated. The artillery standard is shown in **279**. Cavalry standards of the period are illustrated by **134**. Volunteers, guerrillas etc., fighting the French from 1809–14, had flags of their own design, the majority bearing religious emblems or patriotic slogans. Their fields were almost invariably white.

Size: infantry, *circa* 140 cm square.

280–285. Polish colours and standards

The Polish legions which fought in Italy in 1797 carried colours of the type illustrated by **280**. The survivors were formed into the Legion of the Vistula in 1807 and carried colours of the type shown by **281**. The lancers of the legion received in 1800 standards of the pattern shown in **280** and carried these until at least 1810, never receiving an eagle.

In the Duchy of Warsaw the regiments received silver eagles of the style illustrated by Fig. 20. Some had crowns and the bases were usually painted blue with gold lettering. The colours are based on surviving colours taken by the Russians: their size varies – 13th Infantry, 69 by 77 cm; 14th Infantry, 56 by 77 cm; 15th Lancers 60 by 61 cm. The 1st Chasseurs à Cheval carried a crimson standard with a silver eagle in the centre and a silver fringe. Above the eagle was the word LEGIAL and below it 1 PULK

LEKKI IAZDV. Its size was 66 by 74 cm. For colours carried until 1794 see **202** and **203**.

286. France: Régt Irlandais

This regiment was presented in 1804 with the colour illustrated. The reverse was similar but carried in the centre LIBERTÉ / DES / CONSCIENCES / INDÉ-PENDANCE/DE L'IRLANDE surrounded

Fig. 20. Eagle for Duchy of Warsaw infantry.

by a yellow border charged with green wreaths. In 1811 the regiment became the 3rd Foreign Regt. The 2nd, 3rd and 5th Battalions' colours of this date are known to have been green but with only one large golden harp in the centre. It is not known when the new pattern was introduced. For the 1813 campaign in Germany the regiment received ordinary French colours, see **248**.

Size: 80 cm square.

287. Holland: 5th Line Infantry

The colour of an infantry regiment during the Kingdom of Holland (1806–10) under Prince Louis Bonaparte. The illustration is a reconstruction based on an illustration in Ford's work, and the detail of the lion is by no means clear. Ford shows the lion standing and facing right, though it should be facing left. The reverse is of the same style but in place of the lion bears the inscription DE KONING/AAN/ HET 5de REGIMENT/INFANTERIE VAN LINIE/2de BATAILLON. Other regiments may have carried similar colours. When Louis relinquished the throne and Holland was annexed by France, the regiments carried colours of the French pattern; see **247–248**.

Size: 80 cm square.

288. Sweden: Royal Swedois Regt

The Royal Swedois was not a Free Corps but part of the Swedish Army under the former French Marshal Bernadotte, Crown Prince of Sweden from 1810. It was raised in Germany in December 1813 by a French émigré and fought in the Leipzig campaign against Napoleon and in the invasion of Norway in 1814, being disbanded that December. The colour is interesting because it follows the old French Royal Army style of a white cross overall, with the royal arms of France in the centre.

289. Switzerland: infantry colours

Six demi-brigades of infantry were formed in November 1798 at the demand of the French government. The reverse of the pattern for infantry colours is illustrated here; the obverse is shown by Fig. 21. Centre emblems were the same for all demi-brigades but the geometric pattern round them and the colours of the four corners, varied from unit to unit.

Size: 163 cm square.

Fig. 21

290. Army of Condé: Grenadiers de Bourbon

This army consisted of French émigrés under the command of the Compte de Condé and at first served the British. In September 1797 the army was transferred to Russian service and was re-equipped and re-organized on Russian lines. The colour illustrated (obverse and reverse) is clearly of Russian pattern but bears the fleur-de-lis of Royalist France.

Size: 137·5 cm square.

291. Émigré Regt: Dragons d'Enghien

This regiment carried one colonel's standard and four squadron standards of the pattern illustrated from May 1798 until 1800. It transferred to the British service as the Chasseurs Britanniques in May 1801. The colonel's standard is illustrated; the other standards were similar but with yellow instead of a White Maltese cross.

WAR OF 1812 1812–1815

292. Britain: 7th Royal Fusiliers
Regimental colour made during the last decade of the eighteenth century by the Royal Princesses of England for their brother the Duke of Kent, colonel of the regiment from 1789–1801. The wreath is most unusual for royal regiments at this time and even more rare is its rich gold embroidery in place of the usual green. The King's colour has the same central emblem but no corner emblems. The colour carried previously, from 1785–95, was more typical of the plain colours being carried by royal regiments, having no wreath and the corner emblems being just the white horse of Hanover standing on a green field.
Size: Length 195 cm. Breadth 180 cm.

293. Britain: 4th West India Regt
Regimental colour carried from *circa* 1795 until just after the Union with Ireland in 1801. The King's colour had the same wreath but bore in its centre only the circular shield of red with G.R./West Indies/4th Regiment (3 lines) upon it with a crown over the shield. The method of showing the regimental number is conjectural. The central emblem was unofficial but the pineapple came to be recognized officially as the regiment's

badge. The regiment was disbanded in 1819.
Size: Length 195 cm. Breadth 180 cm.

294–295. Britain: 4th Foot
Typical plain colours for Royal regiments of this period, the Union wreath not being authorized for Royal regiments and rarely seen on their colours until 1816. (The stave is on the right of **294**, on the left of **295**.) The lion of England badge was awarded in 1747: the honour Peninsula was awarded on 6 April 1815 and would not have appeared on the colours in North America. The method of showing the regiment's number is conjectural. The 1st Battalion arrived back in Europe in time for Waterloo and fought in the La Haye Sainte area, carrying the colours illustrated.
Size: Length 195 cm. Breadth 180 cm.

296–297. Britain: Quebec Militia
Six battalions of militia were raised in Lower Canada, the 6th being allotted garrison duties in Quebec. In 1813 the 6th was given black facings and the regimental colour conforms to the British warrant of

1768, a St George's cross overall on a black field. As in **294**-5, these colours face each other: i.e. **296** shows the reverse of the King's Colour.) The 1st Battalion had blue facings; 2nd, light green; 3rd, yellow; 4th, dark green; 5th, black.

Size: Length 195 cm. Breadth 180 cm.

298-299. U.S.A.: infantry colours

From 1796 the infantry regiments of the U.S. Army were supplied with a blue national colour and a white or yellow regimental colour. The two national colours illustrated show that at this early date there was no standardization. (See also jacket illustration, the army's first national colour of 1787-91.) The colour of the 2nd Infantry (**298**) is said: o have been surrendered at Fort Bowyer. The regimental colour was white and bore on a three part scroll REGI-MENT OF/THE SECOND/US INFANTRY. The scrolls were light blue with gold lettering and edges. The 4th Infantry was organized in 1796 and the national colour illustrated (**299**) is believed to have been taken at Fort Detroit in 1812. The white regimental colour was not of the usual pattern, having a two part scroll of light blue bearing in black letters FOURTH REGIMENT OF INFANTRY, with US in a green wreath above the centre.

300. U.S.A.: 68th James City Light Infantry

The colour of this militia regiment appears to be a combination of the National and Regimental colours of the regular army. On the reverse is a female figure wearing a helmet and carrying in her left hand a white flag with four red stripes. A man sits near her right foot and behind him are stars and a crown. More stars enclose the figure in an inverted U and the regimental designation appears below this emblem. At the top of the colour is VIRGINIA on a blue scroll.

301. U.S.A.: 1st Harford Light Dragoons

One of two flags believed to have been captured at Bladensburg in August 1814 by the 85th Foot. (The other flag is shown by **300**.)

302. U.S.A.: New York Militia Regt

This colour was taken by British forces at Queenston Height in October 1812 and bears the arms of the city of New York. The reverse bears the eagle emblem of the United States.

303. U.S.A.: 1st Regt of Light Artillery

National standard carried by the 1st Regt of Light Artillery from 1808-21. The regiment was organized in 1808 and the standard was probably used in the war of 1812. It is marked First Regt since a 2nd Regt was anticipated. The lettering should be gold.

Size: Length 207·5 cm. Breadth 170 cm.

304. General Miranda's flag

The *Intendencia* of Quito (subsequently Ecuador) revolted against Spanish rule in August 1809 and much fighting took place under the colours illustrated, which appear to have been carried from the first night of the revolt. General Francisco Antonio Miranda and Bolivar succeeded in establishing the Republic of Colombia in 1811 and both used this flag for their armies; it is frequently referred to as Bolivar's flag. The flag became the national flag of Venezuela (1829) and Ecuador (1830) when these states left the republic.

305. Argentina: General Belgrano's flag

The blue and white of the Argentine flag are said to have originated from the blue and white uniforms of the famous Argentine regiment the Patricios, raised in 1806. The flag first appeared on 3 June 1807, supposedly created by General Belgrano. The sun was added in 1813 and the flag is still in use in this form as the war flag, naval ensign and national flag.

306. Uruguay: Artigas' flag

José Gervasio Artigas helped to free the Banda Oriental from the Spanish by 1811 but this was followed by a struggle for freedom from Argentina, during which the first Uruguayan flag was created; the flag illustrated. Soon after achieving freedom from Argentina, Uruguay was invaded by

the Portuguese from Brazil and was annexed to Brazil in 1820. Independence was not achieved until 1828 and during the 1823–8 period the forces of Uruguay carried a flag of three horizontal bands, blue/white/red, with on the central band the motto LIBERTY OR DEATH.

307. Flag of the Andes Army

In 1817 General José de San Martin led an army over the Andes from Argentina to Chile and in 1818 helped that country gain independence from Spain, thus ending a war of independence which had started in 1810. The flag shown was carried by San Martin's army. The Chilean army raised its first flag on 30 September 1812, three horizontal bands, blue/white/yellow. In May 1817 this was changed to blue/white/red and in September the same year the present national flag was adopted. A popular slogan carried on these flags during the long war was POR LA RAZÓN O LA FUERZA; By Right or Might.

308. Peru: General San Martin's flag

After winning freedom for his own country of Argentina and for Chile, in 1820 General San Martin landed in Peru to liberate its people. His forces bore the flag illustrated. However, this proved too difficult to make for the simple means available to the rebels and in 1822 it was changed to a flag of three horizontal bands, red/

white/red with a sun from the arms of San Martin in the centre (see **305**). Confusion on the field of battle with the Spanish red/yellow/red flag (**309**) led to these colours being carried in vertical stripes and when sovereignty was established in 1825 the vertical stripes were kept as the basis for the national flag.

309. Spain: infantry colours

Until 1821 the flags of the Spanish Army followed the patterns of the Napoleonic era (see **134** and **277–279**) but at the end of November of that year there was a mutiny and a decree issued subsequently laid down that in future a bronze standard would be borne instead of a flag, the stave decorated by only a cravat. The revolu-

tion was ended by the battle of Trocadero in August 1823 and on 1 May 1824 the old type of army flags were reinstituted. These were carried through the Carlist War and Civil War. On 13 October 1843 a decree issued by the provisional government stated that the regimental colours would again be of the same colours as the national war flag, i.e. red/yellow/red, with the royal arms in the centre, and around the arms the number and battalion of the regiment in black. In December 1843 another decree added the cross of Burgundy to the royal arms and forbade the embroidering of the arms in gold or silver. These patterns were carried by all arms in the appopriate shape.

Size: (infantry) *circa* 140 cm square.

MEXICAN WARS 1810–1848

310. Fr. Miguel Hidalgo's banner

Mexico's soldier–priest Father Hidalgo raised his standard, most commonly known as the flag of the Virgin of Guadalupe, on 16 September 1810 and so began the revolutionary movement in Mexico against Spanish rule. The wings of the angel at the Virgin's feet are in the colours which later became the Mexican national flag; green/white/red.

311. Fr. José María Morelos' banner

Hidalgo was executed in 1811 but another priest, Fr. Morelos, took up the cause and carried a white banner

bearing in its centre an eagle and snake device which dates from Aztec times and with a border in the colours of the royal house of Montezuma. The eagle and snake device first appeared on Mexican military flags in 1550, for the invasion of Florida.

312. General Iturbide's flag

General Iturbide was sent by the Viceroy of Mexico to put down the revolution but in 1820 he joined the revolutionaries and independence was finally achieved in 1821 by a union of Spaniards, Indians and all those of mixed blood into one nation. The green, white and red stripes of Iturbide's military flags are said to have stood respectively for independence, purity and Spain. The lettering in the oval should be gold. The type of colour illustrated is believed to have been carried from *circa* April 1821 until independence in September that year.

313. Texan flag of 1835
In 1835 the Texans adopted the Mexican tricolour as their flag but omitted the Mexican arms and substituted 1824, at which date Mexico had established herself as a federal republic, independent of Spain. It is believed this flag was flown at the Alamo. In 1836 Texas adopted the Bonnie Blue flag illustrated by **359** (the early form may have had a gold star and fringe) but in 1839 changed to the flag illustrated by **358**.

314. U.S.A.: New Orleans Greys
In November 1835 two companies of volunteers were organized at New Orleans to fight for Texas and on arrival in Texas were presented with the banner illustrated. Some of the Greys fought at the Alamo and their banner flew over that heroic scene. The remainder were later surprised and captured and most of them massacred at Goliad on 27 March 1836. The eagle's head, holding the end of the scroll in its beak, should appear below the sun.

315. U.S.A.: Newport Rifles
Fifty-two volunteers for Texas gathered at Newport, Kentucky in late 1835. The night before they left for Texas a ball was held at which a young lady gave them a long kid glove as a gage; this glove was thereafter carried at the top of their flag stave. The Rifles arrived in Texas in January 1836 and took part in the Battle of San Jacinto as part of the 1st Regt. Their colour had the distinction of being the only flag carried by the Texas forces at that battle and became known as the Battle of San Jacinto Flag.

CRIMEAN WAR 1853-1856

316. Russia: line infantry colours
Under Nicholas I (1825–55) each infantry battalion carried one colour, and the colours of all the infantry regiments were of basically the same design, illustrated here. Colours of St George were awarded to those regiments which had distinguished themselves in battle: these bore inscriptions in gold cyrillic letters round the edges of the field and had the white cross of St George enamelled on the finial instead of the usual Imperial eagle. All Guards regiments had colours of St George. The field of the colours was green for line, yellow for Guards. The line infantry had white 'corners', the Guards were

Preobrajenski, red/white divided; Semenovski, light blue/white; Ismailovski, white; Ieguerski, green/white; Grenadiers, light blue/black; Pavlov, white/black; Finland, green/black; Litov, red/green; Volyn, green. For the line Grenadiers and Carabiniers the corners were: 1st Division, red/white; 2nd, red/black; 3rd, red/yellow. Carabinier colours also had the corners divided from the field by yellow bands 4 cm wide.

Size: 140 cm square.

317. Russia: Kazanski Jägers

Jäger regiments were distinguished by a 40 cm wide band between field and corner colours; light blue for the first regiment in each division, red for the second. The colour illustrated also bears a light blue ribbon awarded to all regiments which had been in existence for 100 years or more, and had a cravat 40 cm wide by 70 cm long. The cravat was light blue for the Guards, red for Line, and at one end bore the monogram of the Czar granting the cravat, at the other the monogram of the Czar who founded the regiment, and along its length the titles of the regiment.

Size: 140 cm square.

318. Russia: Odesski Lancers

All cavalry regiments bore basically similar standards, green for line, yellow for Guards. The Imperial eagle, braid, borders and fringes were in the button colour of the regiment; the corners in the colour allocated to the regiment. In the case of the Guards these were: Chevalier Guards,

Gardes à Cheval and Tsarevitch's Guard Lancers, yellow: Emperor's Guard Cuirassiers and Guard Lancers, blue: Guard Horse Grenadiers, green: Guard Hussars, red.

Size: Length 60 cm. Breadth 52·5 cm.

319. Russia: Akhtirski Hussars

A line cavalry standard of the St George pattern, with jubilee ribbon. A red cravat, edged and lettered in gold, was also carried. Cravat and ribbon were ruled by the same regulations as the infantry (see 316) and the cravat was of the same length as for infantry.

Size: Length 60 cm. Breadth 52·5 cm.

320. Russia: Standard of the Host of Azov

Under Czar Nicholas I the Cossacks were organized into regiments and armies, or Hosts. In 1844, the Host of Azov was awarded the standard illustrated. The Host of the Black Sea was awarded a similar standard in 1843, but with a jubilee ribbon.

Size: 195 cm square.

321. Russia: 1st Regt of the Host of the Black Sea

Individual regiments within a Host carried a banner of the type illustrated. On the reverse the cross was replaced by the Imperial eagle. As with other Russian flags, these could be colours of St George, and one such is illustrated. The 5th, 6th and 8th Regts appear to have carried similar banners, and the Dunaiski Regt of the Host of Azov also carried a banner of this design and using the same colours.

Size: 167·5 cm. square.

322. Britain: 1st Battalion, Coldstream Guards

In 1844 new regulations were issued for infantry colours. The main points were: regiments bearing Royal, County or other titles were to have these designations on a red circular field within the Union wreath, the number of the regiment in Roman numerals in the centre, and all devices, distinctions and honours, until this time on both colours, were now to be on the regimental colour only.

The Guards had continued to follow regulations laid down in the seventeenth century and still had one colour per company, although usually only two per battalion were taken on campaign. However, in 1834 the colonel's, lieutenant colonel's and major's colours became respectively the 1st or King's Colour of the 1st, 2nd and 3rd Battalions. Captains' colours became the 2nd or Regimental Colours, and company badges were displayed in strict rotation on each new issue of colours. This system has been used until the present day. Illustrated is the colour of the 1st Battalion, with the badge of the 15th Company. This colour was carried by the Guards in the Crimea and the honours Alma, Inkerman and Sevastopol were later added below that for Waterloo.

Size: Length 195 cm. Breadth 180 cm.

323. Britain: 4th Dragoon Guards

A general order of 1834 abolished standards for all light cavalry and the 1844 regulations laid down that Dragoon Guards would henceforth carry standards instead of guidons. Battle honours were to be on the regimental standard only. The 2nd or Regimental Guidon of the 4th Royal Irish Dragoon Guards, *circa* 1830, bore the design illustrated. (The star of the Order of St Patrick was not officially authorized until 1838, when new standards were issued.) The 1st or King's Standard was of crimson damask, fringed gold and crimson, with the Union badge (a rose, thistle and shamrock all on one stalk) in the centre and the royal crown over. Beneath the badge the Peninsula scroll and four corner emblems as illustrated.

Size: Length 102·5 cm. Breadth 67·5 cm.

324. Britain: 55th Foot

Regimental colour of the 55th Westmoreland Regt, issued in 1850 and carried by that regiment up the slopes at Alma. The wreath is noteworthy for its extremely fine workmanship. The Chinese dragon and scroll were awarded for the regiment's part in the China War of 1842.

Size: Length 195 cm. Breadth 180 cm.

325. Britain: 57th Foot

Regimental colour of the 57th Foot, issued in 1853, carried in the Crimea, and retired in 1867. The honours Inkerman and Sevastopol were added later.

Size: Reduced in 1855 to Length 180 cm. Breadth 165 cm.

Reduced again in 1858 to Length 120 cm. Breadth 105 cm.

In 1858 the spear head finial was replaced by one in the form of the Royal Crest, the lion of England standing upon the royal crown. In July 1859 infantry colours were ordered to have fringes, the Queen's colour's fringe to be crimson and gold; the Regimental colour's fringe of gold and the facing colour.

326. France: infantry colours
On 5 March 1848 the government of the 2nd Republic proclaimed that the colours of its army would carry the words LIBERTÉ, EGALITÉ, FRATERNITÉ on a blue/white/red tricolour. Following the coup d'état of 2 December 1851, the 2nd Empire was established and Louis Napoleon became Emperor in 1852. As president, Louis Napoleon

approved the adoption of the symbols of the 1st Empire on the army's flags, and the re-establishment of the eagle. The colour illustrated shows the basic pattern for all infantry colours at this time, and the type carried during the Crimean War. As Emperor, Louis distributed the new eagles to the regiments in Paris on 10 May 1852. Cavalry standards followed the same basic pattern as the infantry colours.

Size: infantry, probably 120 cm square: cavalry, 55 cm square.

327. Sardinia: Royal Piedmont Regt
Prior to 1848 Sardinian troops carried red colours bearing the white cross of Savoy overall, but from 30 June 1848, following the first victories in the war of independence for Italy, all troops within the Sardinian army carried colours of the pattern illustrated.

ITALIAN WARS OF INDEPENDENCE 1848–1862

328–329. Austria: Sovereign's colour for infantry
Obverse (**328**) and reverse (**329**) of the 1859 pattern infantry *Leibfahne* for the Austrian army. The obverse of the 1856 pattern battalion colour was similar but on a yellow field; the only differences were in the ribbons and chains of the orders around the shield on the eagle's breast and slight differences in the form of the eagle's wing and tail feathers. The reverse of the 1856 squadron standard was also of basically the same design, on a

yellow field, but without the smaller shields and again with slight differences in the arrangement of ribbons and chains round the main shield.

Size: infantry, Length 180 cm. Breadth 140 cm: cavalry, (approximate) Length 70 cm. Breadth 63 cm.

330. Duchy of Parma: 1st Battalion of Infantry
Parma, Modena and the Papal States revolted against Austrian rule in 1831,

mainly inspired by Guiseppe Mazzini. This revolt was put down but in June 1859 Parma, Modena and Romagna rose again, the three uniting in the autumn under the title of Emilia. The colour illustrated is of *circa* 1853 and bears the full arms of the Dukes of Parma. The cravat was blue with gold tassels, the cords gold and finial gilt.

331. Two Sicilies: 12th Regt of Infantry

Regimental colour of the 12th (Messina) Regiment in 1852. The stave had a gilt finial and carried a

double cravat with four ends of white silk embroidered in gold.

332-333. Papal States: cavalry standards

The standard of the Papal Carabiniers (**332**), formed in July 1815, bears the tiara and crossed keys of the Pope. This regiment was disbanded in 1831 following political riots against the Pope, but was soon re-formed and survived the collapse of the Papal States to serve a united Italy under a different name. The standard of the Papal Dragoons (**333**), dated *circa* 1865, bears the emblem of Pope Pius IX.

AMERICAN CIVIL WAR 1861–1865

334. U.S.A.: National colour for infantry

Each regiment of infantry in the Union Army carried a National colour and a Regimental colour according to patterns laid down in 1841. The National colour was the Stars and Stripes and at the outbreak of war had thirty-three stars, a thirty-fourth (for Kansas) being added three months later. No stars were dropped for seceding states and by the end of the war there were thirty-five (West Virginia joining the Union in 1863). The arrangement of the stars varied considerably, as did the number of points and their colour, as the regulations were not clear on these subjects. Generally speaking the stars were white or silver, though gold ones did occur, and they were normally five

pointed, although six and seven points occur. During the war they were usually arranged in an oval or in rows as shown. The regimental designation was carried on the central bar and subsequently battle honours were placed on the other bars, see **344**. The stave had a spear head finial and blue and white cords.

Size: Length 195 cm. Breadth 180 cm.

335. U.S.A.: Regimental standard for cavalry

Union cavalry carried one regimental standard per regiment, of the pattern illustrated. This pattern was carried until 1895.

Size: Length 72·5 cm. Breadth 67·5 cm.

Regimental colours for infantry followed the same pattern but were 195 cm in length, 180 cm in breadth. Volunteer infantry regiments often carried a state flag instead of a regimental one.

336–337. U.S.A.: artillery flags
The regimental standard for artillery regiments is illustrated by **336**. The National Standard was of the infantry pattern and size, as shown by **334**. The number of the regiment appeared in the left-hand section of the scroll. Yellow remained the field colour for artillery until 1886, when it was changed to red. (In 1887 the cavalry took on a yellow regimental standard and at the same time was granted a national colour of the Stars and Stripes, although the latter was not actually carried until 1895 when a second order was issued.) Artillery guidons (**337**) were carried by each battery within a regiment and bore the regimental and battery numbers.

338–339. U.S.A.: cavalry guidons
Under the 1834 regulations each cavalry squadron carried a guidon as shown by **338**, bearing the squadron letter. This design was superseded in 1863 by the pattern illustrated by **339**. The 1863 regulation was withdrawn in 1865 and the red/white guidon reintroduced.
Size: Length 102·5 cm (37·5 cm to the fork). Breadth 67·5 cm.

340–343 U.S.A.: command flags
Most of the corps within the Union armies had their own flag: that for the 23rd Corps is illustrated by **340**. Army H.Q.s also had their own flags and **341** illustrates that of the Army of the Potomac. Some individual generals also used flags to indicate their position on the battlefield, particularly in the cavalry, where confusion could be considerable. The guidons of General Sheridan (**342**) and General Custer (**343**) are shown as examples. Custer displayed this guidon from October 1863 to June 1864 as commander of the 2nd (Michigan) Brigade: Sheridan displayed the guidon illustrated from 1864–5 as commander of the Army of the Shenandoah and of the Cavalry Corps of the Army of the Potomac.

344. U.S.A.: 3rd Regt New Jersey Volunteers
National colour of the second 3rd New Jersey Regt, following the pattern of regular units' national colours but bearing the arms of New Jersey. One or possibly two battle honours followed 1st Fredericksburg (the honours shown should be more to the left); this part of the flag having been repaired but lettering not included in that repair.
Size: Length 152 cm. Breadth 143 cm.

345. U.S.A.: 3rd New Jersey Cavalry
State or regimental standard, bearing the arms of New Jersey in the centre. The 'Butterfly Boys', one of the regiment's squadrons, bore a distinctive rectangular standard of dark blue, fringed in gold, with in the centre a

large butterfly in brown and black with white edging to its outspread wings.

Size: Length 152 cm. Breadth 122 cm.

346–348. C.S.A.: National colours
The National flag of the Confederacy was used by the military as a National colour in the same way that Union forces utilized the Stars and Stripes. The 1st National colour (**346**) was adopted on 4 March 1861 and carried a white star for each state in the Confederacy, the number increasing to thirteen as more states joined the C.S.A. The regimental name and/or number was inscribed on the central white bar.

Size: circa Length 90 cm. Breadth 60 cm.

This first National colour became known affectionately as the Stars and Bars but it was not sufficiently outstanding on the battlefield and on 1 May 1863 a 2nd National colour, the Stainless Banner, was adopted (**347**).

Size: circa Length 90 cm. Breadth 45 cm.

However, the 2nd National colour was too easily mistaken for a white flag when hanging limp and on 4 March 1865 the 3rd National colour was adopted (**348**). This was not used in battle, though it may have flown over Richmond.

Size: Length 90 cm. Breadth 60 cm.

349. C.S.A.: Battle flag
This was adopted unofficially from September 1861 as the battle flag of the army but never became the official National flag. It was carried until the end of the war. Variations included the same design but with thirteen or seventeen stars; a white flag with the blue cross and white stars; and a blue flag with a white cross but no stars (Arkansas units). Regimental numbers and/or names were inscribed under the cross and battle honours were often carried on the other segments.

Size: 127·5 cm square but some up to 180 cm square are recorded.

350–351. C.S.A.: cavalry guidons
Two of the guidons used by companies of Confederate cavalry within a regiment, **350** being based on the 1st National colour, **351** on the Battle flag. The Battle flag was also used as a cavalry standard, one per regiment (*size:* 75 cm square) and the Texan State flag (**358**) was carried as a cavalry standard in its rectangular form and in guidon form for each company.

Size: (for guidons) Length 102·5 cm (37·5 cm to the fork). Breadth 67·5 cm.

352–353. C.S.A.: artillery standards
Illustrated are two individual standards carried by Stuart's Horse Artillery (**352**) and the Washington Artillery of New Orleans (**353**). The latter carries the Louisiana state emblem of a pelican and her brood. Details of the scrolls are uncertain but the upper scroll was probably the Company one and bore the commander's

name; the bottom one was in Latin, perhaps the regimental motto. The reverse of this standard was a blue saltire on a scarlet field. Most artillery carried the Battle flag as a standard. *Size: circa* 90 cm square.

354-361. C.S.A.: State colours

According to regulations Confederate infantry regiments carried only one colour but in practice many regiments appear to have carried both a National or Battle flag and a state colour. South Carolina carried the state colour illustrated by **354** until her secession from the Union on 20 December 1861; thereafter South Carolina regiments carried the state colour illustrated by **355.** North Carolina regiments carried a state colour as illustrated by **356,** with the regiment's designation on the white part of the colour. **357** is the regimental or state colour carried by the Florida Independent Blues Company: this was an individual flag, not one carried by all regiments from Florida. **358** shows the Texas state colour, adopted 25 January 1839, and carried by most Texan regiments, including the cavalry. **359** shows the equally famous Bonnie Blue flag, which was first adopted in 1836. The Louisiana state colour is illustrated by **360,** and the Virginia state colour by **361.** The motto shown on **360** is that borne on the state flag; the motto on regimental colours was in Latin, but possibly with the same meaning.

AUSTRO-PRUSSIAN AND FRANCO-PRUSSIAN WARS 1866 AND 1870-1871

362. Austria: Sovereign's standard for cavalry

The obverse of the *Leibstandarte* for cavalry regiments from 1768 until 1898. The reverse bore the Imperial eagle.
Size: (approximate) Length 70 cm. Breadth 63 cm.

363. Prussia: Guard Grenadier Regts

The 1860 pattern for Garde-Grenadier Regts, carried by the 1st, 2nd and Fusilier Battalions of the Regiments Elisabeth and Augusta. The Prussian Army was reorganized in 1860 and many colours of this period still bear

the cypher of Friedrich Wilhelm III and Friedrich Wilhelm IV, even though the king was now Wilhelm I.
Size: Length 140 cm. Breadth 120 cm.

364. Prussia: infantry colours

The *Ordinärfahne* illustrated was carried by line infantry battalions from 1828-81. (The Maltese cross should be more pronounced but, unlike other Prussian colours, in this pattern the white 'corners' came to a point at the wreath, not at a hidden point behind the central emblem.) Regiments entitled to the honour Colberg (Grenadier Regts 8 and 9) had an oval light-blue shield edged in gold and bearing COLBERG 1807 in gold, just below the central emblem.

Size: Length 140 cm. Breadth 120 cm.

365. Prussia: cavalry standards

The illustration shows the basic pattern for line cavalry standards issued in 1860 and carried by the following regiments: 5th to 8th Dragoon Regts, 1861–1918: 9th to 16th Dragoon Regts, 1867–1918: 13th to 16th Hussar Regts, 1867–1918: 9th to 12th Uhlan Regts, 1861–1918: 13th to 16th Uhlan Regts, 1867–1918.

366. France: Breton Seamen's flag

During these wars French regiments carried the same pattern colours as illustrated for the Crimean War (**326**). The colour illustrated was carried by 14,000 Breton seamen, mobilized to defend Paris during the war with Prussia: this was the first occasion on which the ermine of Brittany was used as a symbol for Brittany and not purely as a ducal coat of arms or banner. After the abdication of Napoleon III on 22 October 1870, these men were known as the Breton Army and later as the Forces of Brittany.

367. France: Alsatian irregulars

This flag was surrendered by Alsatian irregulars when they were in-

terned during the Franco-Prussian war. The rose is the coat of arms of the town of Hagenau in Lower Alsace and dates from the fourteenth century.

In March 1871 the old colours of the French Army were abolished. New colours were described in decrees of 5 July and 5 August that same year as being of the same size as before, without fringe, cravat or any symbols of the Empire, and the eagles replaced by a lance head. This new pattern was therefore basically as

Fig. 22

shown by **326** but without the corner emblems. In 1879 the size was reduced to 90 cm square for infantry without a fringe, and 64 cm square for cavalry, with one flag per regiment. On 14 July 1880 the pattern illustrated by Fig. 22 was instituted and this pattern has remained in use to the present day. The obverse bears the name of the regiment and RÉPUBLIQUE FRANÇAISE across the centre.

368. Germany: 3rd Battalion Marine Infantry

The German Marine Infantry originated from the Marine Corps of 1849. The 3rd Battalion was raised in, Tsingtao in China in June 1898, garrisoned at Kiatschau, with a home depot at Cuxhaven. Detachments from the battalion took part in the defence of Peking. The colours of the 1st and 2nd Battalions were identical except for the battalion numbers at the corners (under the cypher). Detachments of these two battalions, formed in 1889 from a single battalion raised in 1852, served in the Boxer Rebellion and wars in South West Africa in 1904.

369. Germany: Bavarian infantry colours

In 1841 Ludwig I introduced a new infantry pattern, the same on both sides. The colour illustrated dates from the 1890s but is identical to the 1841 pattern except the earlier colours had green oak wreaths surrounding the corner cyphers of Ludwig II (1864–86). During the period 1866–71 Bavarian cuirassier regiments carried a *Leibstandarte* of white with gold embroidery and fringes, bearing on one side the initials MJK within laurel wreaths. An *ordinärstandarte* was issued but not carried in the field and this was in any case withdrawn in 1872.

370. Germany: Oldenburg infantry colours

The basic pattern for infantry colours of Oldenburg infantry, in this case the 91st Regt, and dating from the 1890s.

371. Russia: infantry colours, 1857

The basic pattern for Grenadier and Line Infantry regiments, issued in 1857. The inscriptions at the edges indicate it is a St George colour, the inscriptions being honours. There is also a jubilee ribbon on this example, a colour of the Sevski or 34th Regt. Most Grenadier and Line regiments appear to have had dark green colours, though tirailleurs bore strawberry ones. A white or colonel's colour was also carried by each regiment.

372. Russia: infantry colours, 1883

The reverse of the 1883 Line Infantry pattern, in this case the colour of the 19th Kostromski Regt. The braid of the border was in the button colour of the regiment; the border and field in the colour allotted to the regiment; and the inner embroidery (the red parts in the example illustrated) in the same colour as the border and field except where this was white, in which case red was used, as here. The obverse bore inscriptions in cyrillic lettering in the four border panels, geometric designs at the corners, as shown in **373**, and in the central panel the figures of two saints, with above them a small cloud from which emerges the upper body and head of a third saint. The outer border is as the reverse. A white colour was also carried.

373. Russia: Army of the Urals
Issued to the Cossack Army of the Urals on 5 June 1884, this banner follows the same basic pattern as the line infantry. The Army of Kuban also followed this pattern but with different religious figures in the centre panel.

374. Africa: standard of the Bey of Tunisia
In the centre is the sword of Muhammad Ali, above and below it the traditional Islamic symbols of crescents and stars (although to be correct the stars are shown as rowels, i.e. stars with a central perforation). The Bey ruled Tunisia under the Sultan of Istanbul but had considerable autonomy until Tunisia became a French protectorate in 1881. At the end of the nineteenth century there was a French army of occupation of about 20,000 and a native 'army' of about 600.

375. Africa: Tunisian flag
One of several Tunisian flags captured by French marines in 1881. The stave sleeve was of blue cloth.
Size: Length 185 cm. Breadth 115 cm.

The others were as shown but with a red sleeve: two yellow bands separated by one of violet with a red sleeve: two green bands separated by one of violet with a yellow sleeve: two green bands separated by one of red with a red sleeve.

376. China: General's pennant
The personal pennant of the Chinese general Ta-chan, captured by the French at Bac-ninh (Tongking) on 12 March 1884. The pennant was flown above a large square standard of red cotton with a black border, in the centre some Chinese characters also in black. Similar pennants were captured in 1883 and at Tongking in 1884, either of cotton or wool, and all bearing Chinese characters as their main design. Some were of triangular shape, including that for the artillery.

377. Sudanese standard
Standard taken from the forces of Osman Digna at the battle of Tamaai on 13 March 1884, during the first Sudanese campaign.

(From a painting of Tamaai by G. D. Giles.)

378. Dahomey: standard of King Behazin
This standard was found on 18 November 1892 at Abomcy, the capital of the native kingdom of Dahomey, after the king had escaped from the French expeditionary corps which occupied his capital on the 17th. The title below the main emblem is in Portuguese.

379. Africa: Mahdi's flag

Allegedly the flag of Muhammad Ahmad (the Mahdi or Guide), used during his Jihad or Holy War of 1881–5. Each of his five chief lieutenants had similar flags, one each of black, white, red, green and yellow. Except for the final sentence the inscription on the flags was as for the Mahdi's: 'O God, O Merciful One, O Compassionate One, O Living One, O Subsisting One, O Lord of Majesty and Honour. There is no god but God. Muhammad is the Apostle of God. Muhammad al-Mahdi is the Successor of the Apostle of God. Ahmad al-Rifa'i is the Saint of God.' The flag illustrated may have been hung lengthways, as a gonfannon, as on the original the stave sleeve is at the left of our illustration.

380. Transvaal: Free Corps of Krügersdorp

The Boers did not carry flags into battle but some units did have flags and one such is illustrated, the flag of the Freiwilligen-Korps von Krügersdorp. The colours of the state troops were virtually the same but the wagon in the central emblem was slightly different.

381–385. India: infantry colours

In 1858 the British Crown took over from the East India Company the administration of India and with it the control of the Indian military forces. Since that date therefore the colours of Indian regiments have in general conformed to the British regulations. In fact designs for new colours for the Indian regiments were subsequently submitted to the Inspector of Colours in London and the colours illustrated are taken from the actual patterns drawn up by the College of Arms and approved by the Adjutant General.

The Queen's and Regimental Colours of the 106th Bombay Light Infantry (**381** and **382**) were issued in 1867. The Queen's Colour of the 27th Bombay Native Light Infantry or 1st Belooch (**383**) was issued in 1877. The regimental colour followed the pattern shown by **382** except there was only one honour on each horizontal arm of the cross, i.e. Delhi (left) and Abyssinia (right), and the centre device bore xxvii with BOMBAY NATIVE LIGHT INFANTRY or 1st BELOOCH around it. These two regimental colours illustrate the pattern for regiments with white or red facings.

The regimental colour of the 108th Madras Infantry (**384**) illustrates the regimental colour for other regiments. The Queen's Colour was the Union with a crown and cviii in the centre. Both were issued in 1867.

The regimental colour of the 2nd Punjab Infantry (**385**) illustrates the pattern for regiments with black facings and is an early example of the Union canton being omitted, a regulation issued in 1881. The Queen's Colour was the Union with the crown and central device repeated, minus the wreath. Both colours were issued in 1882–3.

Sizes: reduced in 1868 to Length 112·5 cm. Breadth 90 cm.

386. India: 1st Lancers, Hyderabad Contingent

The standards of the five mounted regiments of the Hyderabad Contingent (the Nizam's Army) are believed to have all carried the same design. The standard of the 1st (Lancers) is illustrated: that of the 3rd Regt was red; that of the 4th Regt, green but in guidon form and with the emblems smaller in size. The standards of the 2nd and 5th Regts have not been traced. The inscription reads Allah-o-Akbar: the bottom numeral 1 is repeated above in Persian form. The Persian 1 appears on the 4th Regt's guidon but the bottom numeral is 4. The motto appears to have been adopted by the Hyderabad Contingent in general, including the infantry.

387-390. Britain: infantry colours

Several changes occurred in British colours from 1881: the small Union canton was dropped from regimental colours; the regimental colour was to be in the facing colour of the regiment except for those with white facings (and all English and Welsh regiments now had white facings) which would continue to use the St George's cross overall; territorial titles would be included in the central device; the Union wreath to appear only on the regimental colour; the number of the battalion to appear in the canton; and the colours of the 1st and 2nd Battalions only to carry authorized badges and mottoes. As British colours were not carried in action after 1881 (except for an isolated example) these last changes are academic so far as this book is concerned.

The regimental colour of the 73rd Highlanders (387) dates from 1861 and illustrates a colour before the 1881 changes, and also the colour of a regiment without a territorial designation or other title. 388 illustrates the Queen's colour of the 1st Battalion, Grenadier Guards, made in 1867. It is interesting to note this is virtually the colonel's colour of the seventeenth century. The correct arrangement of badges, honours and the central device and wreath is illustrated by the regimental colour of the 27th Inniskilling Regt (389) made in 1869. This is typical of the regimental colours carried during the colonial period. The white horse badge of the House of Hanover was a rare honour for an infantry regiment.

The regimental colour of the 1st Battalion, Royal Welch Fusiliers (390), presented in 1880, is a final example of a regimental colour just before the 1881 changes. The honours Ramillies, Blenheim and Oudenarde were added above the crown *circa* 1882, and Malplaquet and Dettingen above Minden at the same date.

391-392. South Africa: colours and standards

Illustrated are the regimental standard of Weatherley's Horse (391), made by the ladies of Pretoria and issued to the regiment in 1879, and the regimental colour of the Uitenhage Volunteer Rifles (392), carried from 1892 until 1913, when the regiment was disbanded. The colour of the fringe in 391 is not known by the author.

Sizes: (infantry) Length 112·5 cm. Breadth 90 cm. (cavalry) Length 79 cm. Breadth 60 cm.

Examples of Spanish, Italian, French and United States of America colours for the colonial period have not been included here as the flags described for earlier periods were still in use to the end of the nineteenth century. For Spain see **309**; for Italy **327**; for France **366** and **367**; for U.S.A. **334** and **336–339**.

INDEX

Arranged alphabetically by countries, sub-divided into arm of service, with individual regiments listed in alphabetical order under each sub-heading. The reference number is that used for both illustration and plate description except when it appears in italics, when it is for a flag described only in the text and not illustrated in colour. For regiments in foreign service see under the country they served.

BRUNSWICK

CHILE

CHINA

FRIEDLAND-MECKLENBURG

Infantry

Berchtold von Waldstein's Regt	17th c.	2
Maximilian von Waldstein's Regt	17th c.	2
Wallenstein's Life Regt	17th c.	2

GERMANY
(See also Holy Roman Empire and various states.)

Infantry

Marine Infantry	late 19th c.	368

HESSE

Cavalry

standard	17th c.	4

HESSE-CASSEL

Guard Infantry

Garde Grenadiers	late 18th c.	218–19
Leib du Corps	late 18th c.	219

Line Infantry

Bunan's Regt	late 18th c.	218–19
colours	late 18th c.	218–19
Heldring's Regt	late 18th c.	218–19
Hyne's Regt	late 18th c.	218–19
Jäger Regt	late 18th c.	218–19
Knyphausen Regt	late 18th c.	218–19
Kreis Regt	late 18th c.	218–19
Mirbach Regt	late 18th c.	218–19
Prinz Carl Regt	late 18th c.	218
Stein's Regt	late 18th c.	218–19

HESSE-HANAU

Infantry

Erbprinz Regt	late 18th c.	216

HOLLAND

Infantry

County of Holland colour	17th c.	96
Lewenhaupt's Regt	17th c.	95
Line Regts	1806–10	287

HOLY ROMAN EMPIRE
(See also various states.)

Archduke Leopold's guidon	17th c.	3
Cavalry		
Strasbourg mounted burger company	17th c.	78
Infantry		
Balkan irregulars	17th c.	2
colours	17th c.	3, 98
Lübecker Burgerwehr	18th c.	140

HUNGARY (See Austria)

INDIA

French European units:		
Corps in service of Tippoo Sahib	18th c.	192
infantry colour	18th c.	193
Honourable East India Company;		
Bengal Army	18th c.	*188–90*
Bengal Native Infantry	18th c.	*188–90*
Madras Army	18th c.	*188–90*
Indian Army; Cavalry		
1st Lancers, Hyderabad Contingent	late 19th c.	386
3rd Lancers, Hyderabad Contingent	late 19th c.	*386*
4th Lancers, Hyderabad Contingent	late 19th c.	*386*
Infantry		
colours	19th c.	*381–5*
27th Bombay Light Infantry	late 19th c.	383
106th Bombay Light Infantry	late 19th c.	*381–2*
108th Madras Infantry	late 19th c.	384
2nd Punjab Infantry	late 19th c.	385

Melilla	18th c.	136
Valencia	18th c.	137
Volunteers	18th–19th c.	277–9
Waterford (Irish) Regt	18th c.	124

SUDAN

Osman Digna flag	late 19th c.	377
Mahdi's flag	late 19th c.	379
Mahdi's lieutenants' flags	late 19th c.	*379*

SWEDEN

Artillery		
standard	18th c.	110
Dragoons		
guidon	17th c.	58
Guard Cavalry		
H.M. Life Guards	17th c.	81
Carl X's Life Regt	17th c.	33, 57
Carl XI's Life Regt,		
Västermanland Company	17th c.	82
Line Cavalry		
Baner's Regt	17th c.	15
Östergötland Regt	17th c.	*85*
Västgöta Regt	17th c.	85
Viborg Regt	17th c.	67
Guard Infantry		
H.M. German Life Regt	17th c.	83–4
Carl XI's German Guard	17th c.	34, 75
Line Infantry		
colours	17th c.	57–8
	18th c.	*110*
Baner's Life Regt	17th c.	14
Forbes' Regt	17th c.	16
von Liebenstein's German Regt	17th c.	31
Magnus de la Gardie's Life Regt	17th c.	32
Monroe's Regt	17th c.	13
Närke-Värmlands Regt	17th c.	86
Östgöta Regt	17th c.	*86*